ROUTLEDGE LIBRARY EDITIONS: WW2

Volume 25

PSYCHOLOGY AND THE SOLDIER

PSYCHOLOGY AND THE SOLDIER
The Art of Leadership

NORMAN COPELAND

LONDON AND NEW YORK

This edition first published in 2022
by Routledge
2 Park Square, Milton Park, Abingdon, Oxon OX14 4RN

and by Routledge
605 Third Avenue, New York, NY 10158

Routledge is an imprint of the Taylor & Francis Group, an informa business

First published in 1944 by George Allen & Unwin Ltd

All rights reserved. No part of this book may be reprinted or reproduced or utilised in any form or by any electronic, mechanical, or other means, now known or hereafter invented, including photocopying and recording, or in any information storage or retrieval system, without permission in writing from the publishers.

Trademark notice: Product or corporate names may be trademarks or registered trademarks, and are used only for identification and explanation without intent to infringe.

British Library Cataloguing in Publication Data
A catalogue record for this book is available from the British Library

ISBN: 978-1-03-201217-9 (Set)
ISBN: 978-1-00-319367-8 (Set) (ebk)
ISBN: 978-1-03-210227-6 (Volume 25) (hbk)
ISBN: 978-1-03-210236-8 (Volume 25) (pbk)
ISBN: 978-1-00-321432-8 (Volume 25) (ebk)

DOI: 10.4324/9781003214328

Publisher's Note
The publisher has gone to great lengths to ensure the quality of this reprint but points out that some imperfections in the original copies may be apparent.

Disclaimer
The publisher has made every effort to trace copyright holders and would welcome correspondence from those they have been unable to trace.

PSYCHOLOGY AND THE SOLDIER

THE ART OF LEADERSHIP

PSYCHOLOGY AND THE SOLDIER

THE ART OF LEADERSHIP

by

NORMAN COPELAND

London
George Allen & Unwin Ltd
Museum Street

FIRST PUBLISHED IN 1944

ALL RIGHTS RESERVED

TO
MY FATHER

THE PAPER AND BINDING OF THIS
BOOK CONFORM TO THE AUTHORIZED
ECONOMY STANDARD

PRINTED IN GREAT BRITAIN
in 11-point Plantin Type
BY UNWIN BROTHERS LIMITED
WOKING

FOREWORD

by

GENERAL SIR WALTER KIRKE, G.C.B., C.M.G., D.S.O., D.L.

Psychology and leadership are subjects on which it is dangerous to dogmatize, and my only excuse for this Foreword is that the writer and I served together some years ago.

Psychology as a science is a comparatively new subject, certainly so far as the Army is concerned. This is not to say that the necessity for its study has not always existed, nor that the successful leader has not unconsciously studied it throughout his service.

A more debatable point, perhaps, is whether the soldier, as such, *has* a special psychology of his own. The average civilian would probably take the view that he has, but personally, I do not agree. The soldier—even the long service soldier—is not in any way an exceptional being. As Kipling put it:

> "We aren't no thin red 'eroes, and we aren't no blackguards too,
> But single men in barracks most remarkable like you."

whilst the conscripted soldier provides a cross section of the English, Scotch and Welsh races, to be found in no other profession or occupation.

But where there is a marked difference between military and civil life in the opportunities of observing and influencing a man's character, outlook and ideals. As compared with the civilian employer, the officer has all the advantages of a master at a boarding-school over a day-school teacher. He is in continuous contact with his men, and can enter into every aspect of their lives. His interest in their private affairs will be welcomed, whereas in civil life it might be resented. In pre-war days, I was greatly struck by this difference between the regular Army's outlook in this matter as compared with the civilian point of view, represented by the average Territorial soldier. To suggestions to Territorial Army officers that they should know all about their men's civil employment and take a personal interest in their circumstances, I frequently received the answer that the men would regard this as prying into their private affairs and would not like it.

This is probably the explanation for the criticism widely directed against the new type of officer who came in with conscription, to the effect that he did not take sufficient interest in either the collective or individual comfort and welfare of his men. The reason, no doubt, was that he feared it might be resented.

The first endeavour of the officer should be to obtain the confidence of his men to such an extent that they will regard his interest in their personal affairs not as an intrusion but as a compliment, and Mr. Copeland gives a number of hints as to how this happy situation may be achieved, such as "a man's name is to him the most important thing in the English language," "hanging about is the curse of the British Army," and many more shrewd comments of the same kind, to which I would add "be fond of your men; it is easy; they are grand fellows."

On the all-important subject of discipline, and of methods of obtaining it, the author has some wise remarks to make, which carry all the more weight as coming from an unbiassed observer. He also stresses the importance of Regimental history and tradition as potent aids to morale; and in this connection excessive reticence in regard to names of

Units, which have done great deeds, is much to be deprecated as injuriously affecting the prestige, and therefore the morale, of the Army.

No less interesting and instructive are the chapters which deal with leadership, particularly for young officers, who, it is hoped, will study and profit from them. The author stresses the importance of being able to talk, going so far as to say that no one can hope to be a great leader who cannot do so. This may be true in civil or political life, but that it applies to the Army would be questioned by many.

Foch and Nivelle were fine speakers, and indeed the latter owed his appointment as supreme commander to his ability to explain technical matters to politicians in non-technical language; but Joffre was the reverse. Haig was almost inarticulate, and Wavell wastes no words. On the other hand, Mr. Copeland's opinion finds support in the large proportion of men of Irish extraction in our high commands to-day—Dill, Gort, Brooke, Alexander, Pile, Montgomery—for the Irishman is proverbially as ready in speech as he is in action.

Times have changed since the day when subalterns were expected to be seen and not heard, and we may agree that ability to talk well is an asset which all should endeavour to acquire. But whether in peace or war, it is deeds rather than words that count in the Army, and something much more than a ready tongue is required of a leader.

The author disagrees with the theory that leaders are born and not made, and each of us has his own reminiscences on which to form an opinion.

How many of our schoolboy leaders have emerged as such in later life? Perhaps we admired them for the wrong qualities, or placed too great importance on proficiency at games, but the fact remains that they appeared to us at any rate to be "born leaders." Most of us will, I think, agree that an equal or greater number of boys, who showed no particular signs of future greatness, have in fact emerged in later life as leaders, and this should encourage every young officer to try, and keep on trying, for to the trier nothing is impossible.

After all, what is it that the average man wants? Surely, to belong to a good show; the best show if possible, whether it be the 8th Platoon, the 8th Battalion, or the 8th Army. In peacetime the reward of success is the respect of his fellows; in war it is the commendation and admiration of a far wider audience, with the added inducement of getting the best return for risking his life.

He wants as his leader the man who is most competent to lead him to success, or, at the worst, to enable him to sell his life to the best advantage; in other words, the most efficient officer. The author stresses the point that there is no short cut to successful leadership, the stages being through knowledge to efficiency, resulting in self-confidence, which is the essential ingredient leading to conviction, and thence to enthusiasm.

To such a man British soldiers will give unwavering loyalty and unstinted service. They will regard even his foibles and eccentricities as lovable and laudable, and they will never let him down.

W. KIRKE

August 30, 1943

CONTENTS

	PAGE
FOREWORD	5
CHAPTER	
I. THE ATTRIBUTES OF A LEADER	11
II. CHARACTER AND PERSONALITY	15
III. PRESTIGE	20
IV. PERSONALITY AND SPEECH	25
V. THE PSYCHOLOGY OF INSTRUCTION	29
VI. EXAMPLE	35
VII. WHAT'S IN A NAME?	39
VIII. THE PSYCHOLOGY OF LEADERSHIP	44
IX. CARE OF MEN	49
X. TEAM SPIRIT	55
XI. MORALE: THE SECRET WEAPON	63
XII. FEAR	72
XIII. THE PSYCHOLOGY OF DISCIPLINE	79
XIV. IDEALS	89

"An Army of Harts led by a Lion, is better than an Army of Lions led by a Hart."

>THE SOULDIERS CATECHISME
>1644

CHAPTER ONE

THE ATTRIBUTES OF A LEADER

Leadership is the art of dealing with human nature. To be more explicit, it is the art of influencing a body of people, by persuasion or example, to follow a line of action. It must never be confused with *drivership*—to coin a word—which is the art of compelling a body of people, by intimidation or force, to follow a line of action. The man who believes he will get the best out of his subordinates by "putting the fear of God into them" ought not to be at large. Certainly he ought never to be allowed to exercise authority over man or beast. It is just as important that the subordinate should have confidence in himself as that he should have confidence in his leader, for self-confidence is essential to morale. The truly great leader is one who, by his own high example, inspires his followers with such an outstanding degree of self-confidence that they will carry out quickly, cheerfully and thoroughly whatever duties they are called upon to perform, or which may suggest themselves to individual initiative.

The life of an army illustrates better than that of any other group the influence of leadership. A Commander-in-Chief may be a general of outstanding intellectual ability, and he may work out a plan of campaign that is perfect in every detail. But in the day of battle it is the fighting spirit of his troops that decides the issue. It is accepted that in warfare "Moral force to the physical"—that is numbers, armament and training—"is as three to one." Indeed, no weapon has ever been invented, and no plan of defence has ever been thought out, that can subdue the fighting spirit of a well-led army. And in these days of large forces and prolonged struggles the development of the fighting spirit depends not upon the generals—but upon the corporals, sergeants, subalterns, captains, majors and colonels. It is the part of these subordinate commanders to reflect the attributes and talents of their Commander-in-Chief, and to do this they must be able to exercise the art of leadership. And further, no well-organized army can afford to dispense with the initiative of the subordinate leaders, for it is the determining factor in modern war.

In the days of the great Napoleon a veteran sergeant said to a young soldier one morning, "Boy, the Emperor is come; the Emperor is here." The young soldier asked, "How do you know it? I have been down to the General's quarters, and I have seen and heard nothing." The sergeant answered, "I know he must be here. You don't seem to understand, but can't you see that all the world is up and stirring? Look at those expresses galloping along the road. Everything is moving. Our enemies have no need of their spectacles to see if he is with us. They will find out soon enough." The sergeant was proved to be right. He was a veteran and knew the signs. Napoleon was a man of action, and that attribute was reflected in his subordinates.

The successful leader must stand in a certain relation to the group which he leads. He must be in sympathy with it —in tune with it—and yet in advance of it. To be in sympathy with it he must be a man of character and personality; and to be in advance of it he must possess these attributes in an exceptional degree.

The words *character* and *personality* are often used as though they were synonymous. They are not.

A distinguished American psychiatrist, Dr. Henry Link, has drawn the distinction by defining a man of character as one who possesses the social virtues: he is industrious, conscientious, honest, true to his word, and steady in his habits. He may nevertheless be a dull and uninspiring individual, and completely lacking in what we mean when we say that a man has a good personality. Dr. Link then proceeds to define personality: "Personality is the extent to which the individual can convert his abilities and energies into habits and actions which successfully influence other people."

That definition is so very important that it is worth repeating:

"Personality is the extent to which the individual can convert his abilities and energies into habits and actions which successfully influence other people."

Other things being equal, a man of average intelligence who can play the piano, or drive a motor car, has more potential personality than a man of equal intelligence who can do neither. "Personality is the effect of acquired skill, both in work and in play, which gives the individual the power to attract and influence others." If a man only learns to balance a bottle on the end of his nose he will have increased the effect of his personality.

"An outstanding personality," to quote Dr. Link, "requires not only a variety of skills, but relative superiority in a few fields and distinct superiority in one. The chief superiority should be in a vocational field, and the others in the field of sports, hobbies and the social arts."

In other words, a leader must first have a good general knowledge of his job. Second, he should be a specialist at some branch of his job. And third, his mind should be flexible and comprehensive enough to express itself in interests that are not directly associated with his job.

Sometimes we say of an individual that he has an inferiority complex. Unless we are trained psychologists, with an extensive knowledge of psychological terms, we usually mean that the individual concerned is lacking in personality. And he is lacking in personality because he has failed to cultivate specific habits of success. A man does not succeed because he has personality, but he has personality because he has succeeded.

The individual who has character without personality will generally think in terms only of himself. In the words of a famous cynic, he is an "egoist who has no ego." He can be hard-working, truthful, honest, temperate, religiously-minded—but thoroughly dull, selfish and unpopular. This type, which is by no means uncommon, has proved a source of constant embarrassment to the Christian church, and an occasion of malicious delight to her critics.

It is personality that enables a man to think in terms of other people; and unless he can see things from the other person's point of view he will never make a successful leader. Leadership is a way of life. The individual who aspires to it must change his view-point and his habits. His interests must be focused not on himself but on other people. Selfishness must be replaced by selflessness. Several things will be repeated in this book and this is one of them:

Leadership is a way of life.

"It is the individual who is not interested in his fellow-men who has the greatest difficulties in life and provides the greatest injury to others. It is from among such individuals that all human failures spring." Such was the verdict of the late Dr. Alfred Adler who knew a great deal about human failure and mental misery. A man of personality is one who is interested in his fellows, and the greater his interest the more successful he is likely to be as a leader.

If history proves anything it proves that great leaders are not born but made. Leadership is not the prerogative of a class. Nelson, Napoleon, Cromwell, Wellington, Robert E. Lee, Stonewall Jackson—in what sense was any one of these a *born* leader?

They were great leaders because—in modern slang—they knew their job and they knew it thoroughly. They were well educated in their profession. They possessed the confidence that grows out of efficiency. And with a high standard of professional skill and knowledge they combined a deep personal regard for the men who served them. They had learnt that men can be led only if they are willing to be led; and they went out of their way to make them willing.

CHAPTER TWO

CHARACTER AND PERSONALITY

Success developes personality. Although personality can exist apart from character—and very often does—yet it is true to say that in a leader character must be the foundation of personality. A personality that is not built upon character will never *lead*. And much less will it ever inspire.

The man who has one hundred per cent character and only fifty per cent intelligence is more richly endowed than the man who has one hundred per cent intelligence and only fifty per cent character. It is a common mistake to estimate an individual's ability by his standard of intelligence. The possession of a high intelligence is by no means a guarantee of success in any walk of life. As one psychologist expresses the matter: "For all practical purposes of life, social intelligence wins over abstract intelligence ten to one. Abstract intelligence knows what to do, but social intelligence knows how to get it done."

It is quite common, for example, for a person of high intelligence to be unable to handle his fellow-men, or to be lacking in common sense, or to be in need of drive, whereas another of less intelligence may possess these attributes and succeed where the former fails.

Character is the ability to face facts, and it springs out

of self-discipline. The man who cannot handle himself well will not handle other people any better. "I can't" should not be in the vocabulary of anyone who aspires to be a successful leader. "I can't remember names," "I can't remember faces," "I can't get out of bed in the mornings," "I know I smoke too much, but I can't cut it down"—the individual who persists in allowing himself to indulge in excuses of this nature had better abandon all ambitions of leadership.

Stanley Russell writes: "Down the streets of Portsmouth, more than a hundred years ago, walked a sailor with one arm, one eye, a persistent state of nerves, and unable to tread a ship's deck without being seasick. Indeed, he would probably have been in a home for incurables—were not his name Horatio Nelson. The man's spirit drove the flesh." And the same kind of spirit is available for every man who will go to the trouble of acquiring it.

It is useless for a leader to have a high intelligence and a flashy personality if his character is such that his worthiest subordinates instinctively hold him in contempt. If he is intemperate, if he is not industrious, if he cannot keep his word, if he cannot control his temper, if he is not straight, if he is unjust with a single member of his group, the effect of whatever personality and intelligence he possesses will correspondingly decrease. The leader who is not steady in his habits is often able to attain a measure of popularity with the riff-raff—to whose worst instincts he appeals—for the sufficient reason that he keeps them in countenance; but he will never command the confidence and respect of that large body of decent and reliable men on whom he must ultimately depend for the prompt and efficient execution of his orders.

In order to lead a man must be in advance of his group. He cannot lead from behind or even from the ranks. He can shout and shove, but shouting and shoving are always exhausting and rarely effective. An appointed leader must be accepted by the led as the most able man in the group before he is followed blindly. It is not sufficient that he should have ability. The effect of his personality must be such as to inspire confidence in his ability.

The question is often asked: Can personality be developed? If personality is the reward of success there is simply no limit to its development. Success in some form or other can be achieved every day. A man may succeed in mastering the fiddle, and by doing so he will develop his personality. But unless he has a natural gift for music he might spend his time far more profitably in chopping sticks. It is much wiser and more economical for a man to find out what are his own natural gifts, and to develop and train them. If he has a gift for languages, then, of course, he will study languages. But he should ask himself: How can I make use of this new accomplishment? How can I make it part of my life? A man has no business to go through life dallying with this and that when he does not know all there is to know about the job which provides his bread and butter. The successful leader is a man who has learnt to put first things first.

But no man can be a great, or even a good, leader merely through study. He must possess courage, self-reliance and coolness in danger. These qualities are not derived from education but often they can be developed. Apart from the recreational importance of games they are of definite value in developing a man's powers of leadership. It is impossible to harden the body without at the same time steeling the will. Not only are field games the means of instilling coolness, courage and self-reliance, but they teach a man in a very practical manner that the co-operative efforts of the team are far more effective than the isolated efforts of individuals. Moreover, if a man learns to ride a horse, to play cricket or football, to shoot or fish, to play golf, or even bridge, the effect of his personality will quite definitely increase, for he is able to influence a larger circle of people than before. He has acquired a new accomplishment and added to the general stock of his ability. And as physical relaxation and recreation are essential under the strain and stress of modern life there could be no better way of spending part of one's leisure than by indulging in some form of sport.

In *Generalship: Its Diseases and their Cure*, Major-General J. F. C. Fuller makes a characteristically vigorous attack, which is by no means unjustified, on the "cricket complex." It has inhibited us with "the comfortable theory that to amuse ourselves is the most perfect way of learning to become soldiers." It needs to be pointed out that because a man is a brilliant athlete it by no means follows that he has the qualities which make a leader. He can be an athlete of international reputation, and yet barely half-witted. Athletic ability and intellectual ability do not necessarily go together.

Three points, therefore, ought to be emphasized: (1) Many great leaders have had no aptitude for games; (2) In no circumstances ought games and sports to be allowed to come before work and duty; and (3) The man who has no aptitude for games—who was born with two left hands or two left feet—ought never to be compelled to play them. His sense of failure will react unfavourably on his personality.

In discussing the value of religion in relation to leadership the cynical might well be excused for enquiring whether it is proposed to analyse the attributes of leadership on the level of a Sunday School tract. But the truth must not be shirked for fear of giving offence. That religion can play a large part in the making of a leader no one can deny. The number of devout, God-fearing men who hold high rank in the three fighting services is very striking. It would, however, be more fitting if a regimental officer were allowed to speak on this point. In his *Talks on Leadership*, a book which is familiar to every regular artillery officer, *Basilisk* writes:

"Though a spirit warmed by the fires of religion is not essential to the making of a great leader, yet it is a fact, and if a coincidence then a very striking one, that almost all our great leaders in the field have been pre-eminently religious men. From the Black Prince, Henry V and Cromwell, through Marlborough and Nelson, to that band of Mutiny heroes, John Nicholson, Outram, the Lawrences and Havelock, down to our own time—Lords Wolseley and Roberts, Sir Evelyn Wood and Kitchener—we see the same characteristic. And our American cousins admit it in the persons of their great national leaders, George Washington, Stonewall Jackson and Robert E. Lee. There can be no doubt that the troops respect and trust an officer who without parading his religion does not attempt to hide or disown it. *Cœteris paribus* a religiously disposed officer is the better leader."

The God-fearing leader brings to his job something that others do not possess. He brings faith, and that single attribute is of inestimable value. For faith can accomplish the impossible. Military science said that Wolfe could not capture Quebec. Faith said he could. And faith was right. A precipitous cliff-side was scaled by an armed force, in perfect silence, in the dead of night. Faith had removed another mountain.

A leader must be inspired with the conviction: *I am going to succeed*. The man who becomes a millionaire is a man who will go to more trouble to make sixpence than the ordinary man will take to make a pound. Ask any eminently successful man what he considers the secret of success, and he will reply to this effect: Once you start a job never let go. Keep hard at it till you have accomplished what you set out to do. When you have finished begin something new. Never admit defeat.

The man who becomes an outstanding leader is a man who will go to more trouble to understand and handle a single individual than the ordinary man will take to understand and handle an army. If a man cannot handle a single individual well he will never handle a group any better.

CHAPTER THREE

PRESTIGE

Qualities of leadership are partly natural and partly acquired. That some men can make themselves more readily obeyed than others cannot be denied. In every great leader—as in every other genius—there is some magic quality that defies definition and analysis. How far that particular quality is natural, and how far it is acquired, it is not easy to say; but certainly it is neither completely one nor the other. Nor is it the inheritance of a particular class. The general laws of biology and psychology recognize no favourites.

In *Morale and Its Enemies* Hocking points out that "The relation of command and obedience is not a relation between two individuals: a third and invisible party to the situation is always present—the authority of the state and army." That is true in theory, but in practice the point is of little consequence. Anyone who has exercised command in the services knows very well that personality is more powerful than the *Manual of Military Law*. There is a very great difference between the command of a military officer and that of a civil official. The village constable tells the doctor he drives too fast, and orders him not to do it again. And the doctor obeys. Behind the constable is the authority of a third party—the state—of which he himself is merely the instrument. On another occasion the doctor, in his capacity of medical officer of health, orders the village constable to attend to his drains. And *he* obeys. In giving the order the doctor is the instrument of the same invisible authority which upheld the constable. In each case the actual command belonged to this third party, for it alone had the authority to issue it and the power to enforce obedience.

In the same way when a newly-appointed lance-corporal first gives the order to "Fall in" he is backed by a perfect hierarchy of authority which includes his Sergeant-Major, Company-Commander, Commanding Officer, General Officer Commanding-in-Chief, the Army Council, and both Houses of Parliament. But he will derive little comfort from the knowledge that this imposing array of power is marshalled behind him. His voice will still sound weedy and his knees still knock. He is as much an instrument of the state as the constable or the doctor, yet before he is that he is a member—and the leader—of this very group. He is conscious that his own personality plays the chief part in the transaction, for the very manner in which his order is delivered determines the kind of response which it stimulates.

Nor is that all. He must consider how his subordinates will act when they are beyond the reach of orders, for that is the crucial test of leadership. His command is not an occasional or a temporary affair, but a settled relationship between himself and a group of individuals. When he gives orders to strange individuals who do not belong to his own particular group, then indeed it is the army which is obeyed rather than himself. But within his own group his command must be based upon his own personality, or it is based upon nothing at all. He is not appointed to enforce obedience, but to inspire it.

In an army, at any rate, it is not possible to divorce command from leadership. Every officer or non-commissioned officer who makes the slightest attempt to stand on the army's feet should be elbowed aside and told to stand on his own. There is no divine right of leaders. Even if they are not appointed by popular election at any rate they are acknowledged and maintained by popular consent—or they are not *leaders*, whatever else they may be.

In every army the importance of leadership is recognized, and a system of graded ranks is essential to its organization. Everything is done to give the leaders of each grade the greatest possible prestige: chevrons and badges of rank, salutes, separate messes, red tabs, brass hats, etc. But though much can be done in this way, unless the men appointed as leaders have in some degree the superior qualities required of their position the whole organization will prove of little value.

A leader must have a prestige of his own in addition to that which is conferred upon him by virtue of his rank and appointment, and, more than that, it must be the right kind of prestige. In the eyes of many a man has prestige because he runs three motor-cars. In the eyes of some others he has prestige because he can drink all his friends under the table. Or he may even have a well-merited prestige as a result of being an excellent horseman or a brilliant athlete. But in none of these cases is the prestige of such a nature as to inspire an unequivocal confidence in his leadership. The prestige which is so essential to a leader is moral rather than physical or intellectual: his subordinates want to feel that he has the character, or the will-power, to do the right thing, no matter what the circumstances, and that he can be relied upon at all times.

That is not to say that physical and intellectual prestige are not important. Indeed they are so very important that a leader must take pains to make the best of whatever presence he has, and attend to the least detail of his dress,

If he is small of stature he may take courage from the knowledge that so were many great leaders—including Napoleon and Roberts—who nevertheless knew how to obey and be obeyed. But he should be punctilious in compensating for any natural defects by acquiring new accomplishments. Every leader must endeavour to have his job at his finger tips, and still find time to qualify as a well-informed man of wide interests. He must look alive and alert. If he is naturally diffident he must cultivate an absorbing interest in the social welfare of his group. And if he is naturally assertive he would be wise to train himself in the virtue of humility.

It is commonly supposed that the assertive type makes the best leader, but this is a dangerous illusion. Certainly he knows how to get things done so long as he can give matters his own personal attention. But though he can drive men he can rarely inspire them. He is unable to command all those important extras which subordinates so willingly concede of their own personal initiative to a leader whom they instinctively like. A good leader gets things done with a maximum of willingness and a minimum of effort. The assertive type gets things done, but with a minimum of willingness and a maximum of effort. He would vary the emphasis of Napoleon's aphorism to make it read: *Physical force to the moral is as three to one.* This is bad economy.

A leader must look the part and live the part. He must be thoroughly reliable and efficient. He must be absolutely straight and scrupulously just. He must be courageous, forbearing and generous. He must be able to see everything from the view-point of his subordinates as well as of his superiors. And when all these things have been mellowed by the experience of command, then indeed he may modestly but confidently affirm with the centurion: "I also am a man set under authority, having under me soldiers, and I say unto one, Go, and he goeth; and to another, Come, and he cometh."

But no one will ever make an outstanding leader unless he can talk, for it is chiefly through speech that man expresses his personality. "Among the many forms of the psychological 'it' there is perhaps none so important as oratory—to explain what you want, and to put your verve and enthusiasm over to your hearers." Who thought of that? A leading statesman? A teacher of elocution? A Hollywood film producer? None of these. It comes from General Sir George McMunn, late of the Royal Artillery. Not only is he a great student of history, and a writer of distinction, but he has spent the best part of his life handling regular soldiers—Indian as well as European—and we may take it he knows what he is talking about.

Leadership and command gravitate to the man who can talk. A politician is raised to cabinet rank not because he is strong and silent, but because by his speech he can inspire confidence and arouse enthusiasm. A trade-union leader does not graduate from the workshop because he is a more skilled fitter or carpenter than his work-mates, but because he knows how to express his personality through speech. In every profession the man who can talk coherently and convincingly is instinctively followed. To repeat a statement that was made earlier: Leadership is the art of influencing a body of people, by *persuasion* or example, to follow a line of action. People are persuaded through speech.

The man who has never trained himself to talk will generally regard oratory as a gift which is beyond the reach of all but a favoured few. This, of course, is a mistake. It is as easy for the average man to become an accomplished speaker as to become an accomplished driver of a motor car. The most ready way for anyone who wishes to develop his personality is by teaching himself to talk to his fellow men. There is no magic in speech except in its effect. The ability to speak convincingly is as necessary to a military leader as to any other leader.

Effective speech grows out of constant practice, and the application of a few simple rules. These can best be taught by parable, and that is the method which is adopted in the chapter that follows.

CHAPTER FOUR

PERSONALITY AND SPEECH

Fumbling at his equipment with restless fingers, Lieutenant Haversack gazed vaguely into the middle distance over the heads of his platoon which was drawn up before him. Then he began:

"Er—I want—uh—I want you to pay—er—attention for a moment." (Drops his map case and slowly picks it up.) "Um—this platoon—*Seven platoon*—has—er—been dropped on by the C.O. for a rather sticky job." (Starts fiddling about with his compass.) "Hem—it's this way—er—the bally old Hun has—er—established two what-do-you-call-ems—outposts—on the hill-side over there." (Blows his nose.) "Hem—we have to—er—at any rate we have to try to tackle one of them—and—uh—*Eight platoon* will sort of—er—deal with the other." (Rubs his left eye.) "So see if you can sort of pull yourselves together." (Rubs his right eye.) "Stand still, Jones—you're on parade. Take his name, Sergeant: 'Moving in the ranks.' So we must all sort of do our best—if you know what I mean. I don't think there is anything else."

A hundred yards away Lieutenant Thunderbolt stood confident and erect looking into the eyes of his troops. "Men," he began, "the Commanding Officer has chosen us for a lively mopping-up job. The enemy has established two outposts on the hill-side there. If they are not attended to at once they will give a great deal of trouble. We are going to attend to one of them! *Seven platoon* will attend to the other. You know the drill; we've practised this kind of job scores of times. Lance-corporal Sniffkins and his section will bolt them with hand grenades. Private Mulvaney and his gang will then give them the works with the Bren gun. The rest of us will be placed so as to cut off their retreat. On no account must a single man be allowed to get away. So get stuck into them, and knock the lights out of them. Ready, men? Grand! Good old *Blankshires!* That's the spirit, *Eight platoon!* Let's go!"

One of those platoons carried out the operation with complete success. The other failed. Which platoon succeeded? Which platoon failed? No prizes are offered for the right answers.

When Haversack and Thunderbolt left their Battalion Headquarters they had the same immediate purpose in view. That purpose was to inform their men that they had been detailed for a raid. But the average soldier cannot be expected to work up any great enthusiasm about that. Raiding is a very dangerous business, and those who take part in it often get hurt—or worse. The instinct of self-preservation is very strong, and it is no use trying to fight battles as if there were no such thing. Haversack's technique was wrong from the start. *He failed to look at the matter from the viewpoint of his men.*

Thunderbolt, on the other hand, *began* with the right idea. His purpose was exactly the same as Haversack's, but he adapted his technique to the occasion. He told his men they had been chosen to knock daylight out of the enemy. That was the very thing *Eight platoon* wanted to do: knocking daylight out of the enemy was far more healthy than the enemy knocking daylight out of them. And according to their reasoning the Commanding Officer knew what he was about when he chose *Eight platoon*. Their pride was aroused. They would do what was required.

Next, Haversack's manner was anything but reassuring. His hands were restless, indicating that his nerves were not under control. He avoided looking his men in the face. He appeared from his extraordinary speech to have but a very uncertain grasp of the situation, although actually he may have known it even better than Thunderbolt. He did not suggest that he had formulated any plan to deal with it. He found fault with his men at the very time when he needed all their loyalty and fighting spirit. He gave them the impression that the raid might not succeed, and so aroused their worst fears. How, in such circumstances, could *Seven platoon* do otherwise than fail?

Thunderbolt's presence inspired confidence. He stood erect, and by looking his men straight in the face he was able to inspire them with his own enthusiasm. He did not distract their attention from the matter in hand by fumbling about with his equipment. His speech was brisk and to the point, suggesting that he knew exactly what was required. He brought his men right into the plan of campaign; it was their "party" as well as his. And it was going to succeed. The whole thing was "in the bag" before *Eight platoon* set out. How could they possibly fail?

From this it is possible to set forth certain rules:

(1) To inspire men to effective action it is necessary to propose something *they* want to do.

(2) To inspire confidence a speaker should stand erect, chest high, and look his hearers in the face.

(3) He should know what he is going to say before he starts to say it.

(4) He should ask himself, "Why am I making this speech?" If he does not know, then he should not make it. Every speech must have a definite purpose.

(5) He must not indulge in mannerisms that distract attention.

(6) He must work on the best, and not on the worst, feelings of his hearers.

(7) He should use short words and sentences.

(8) He should endeavour to bring his hearers into his speech.

(9) He must speak up.

(10) He must know when to stop. An effective speech can be spoiled by continuing just a minute too long.

An authority on the art of public speaking, Albert J. Beveridge, has written: "Not one immortal utterance can be produced which contains such expressions as 'I may be wrong', or 'In my humble opinion,' or 'In my judgment.' The great speakers, in their highest moments, have always been so charged with aggressive conviction that they have announced their conclusions as ultimate truths. They speak 'as one having authority,' and therefore 'the common people hear them gladly.' "

To develop his personality and impress it on others it is necessary for a man to be able to talk with fluency and conviction. Men will follow one who can talk. They will not follow one who is dumb. It is a good practice for a Commanding Officer to have all his subordinate officers in conference once a week, and encourage them to *stand up* and talk. There is only one way to learn to swim, and that is to get into the water. And there is only one way to learn to talk, and that is to stand on one's feet and talk. The art of speaking is acquired by speaking.

A convenient method is for the Commanding Officer to ask each officer his opinion about some item on the agenda. At first, many of the younger officers will be nervous and will say no more than that they agree with Major Howitzer or Captain Blunderbuss. But after a time they will realize it is much easier and less embarrassing to give tongue to one's own ideas than to go through life nodding agreement with those of other people. Nervousness goes out, and self-confidence comes in, immediately the novice feels he has a record of successful experiences behind him.

Men have confidence in one who has confidence in himself. It would be absurd to expect them to have confidence in an individual who has no confidence in himself. No one can address his fellow men without revealing to some extent the kind of man he is. His knowledge and ability, his intelligence and personality are all on public show. The wise man will take pains to exhibit them to the best advantage.

CHAPTER FIVE

THE PSYCHOLOGY OF INSTRUCTION

Recently at a military instructional centre a lecturer was interrupted by a voice from the rear of the lecture-room which protested in tones of exasperation, "Louder and funnier!" Needless to say, the disgruntled one was an officer from one of the dominions. We all know from bitter experience how he must have felt, and can envy the moral courage that was able to take such exquisite revenge.

Most officers and non-commissioned officers find themselves called upon to instruct at some time or other. A leader who is a good instructor has obvious advantages over a leader who is a bad instructor. A bad instructor may sometimes begin by evoking pity, but he invariably ends by causing irritation. The man who cannot convey his ideas coherently and convincingly will never make a great leader.

No one can talk interestingly and refreshingly for any

length of time unless he reads, for in reading we acquire words, images and ideas. It is essential for one whose business it is to instruct, no matter what form the instruction takes, to know what is going on in the world. He must know each day's news the day it breaks. The man who does not know what everyone else knows will not be credited with knowing what no one else knows. A definite time should be set aside each day for the reading of newspapers, magazines and books. And every combatant officer should pay regard to the advice of Napoleon: "The only right way of learning the science of war is to read and re-read the campaigns of the great captains." For the beginner these campaigns can best be studied in the pages of biography.

Everyone who sets out to read intelligently will find it profitable to keep a scrap-book, for a great deal of what is read is otherwise forgotten before it can be put to good use. A well-stocked scrap-book will always provide some material for a talk on any subject under the sun.

Although reading is the most ready and fruitful source of ideas and information, yet it should be remembered that ideas and information gleaned from a printed page do not really belong to the reader till they have been mentally digested. And the most valuable method of making acquired ideas and information one's own is to discuss them in conversation. "Conference maketh a ready man," says Bacon, and certainly it is of the highest importance in teaching a man to marshal his facts coherently, and to build up a case that is proof against attack. In conversation, too, we are able to augment our information as well as test the validity of our conclusions.

When preparing material for instructional purposes it is a wise plan always to have much more available than one intends to use. Not only does this give the instructor a feeling of confidence, but if things take an unexpected turn, and they sometimes do, it is easy to adapt oneself to the changed circumstances. The unused material can be used on another occasion.

If the instruction is to take the form of a lecture there are three main methods of preparing it:

(1) *Writing out the lecture and reading it.* Of the three this has the least to commend it, for the instructor is unable to give his attention to the class. The result is that one's hearers soon become bored and restless.

(2) *Writing out the lecture and committing it to memory.* This method has its advantages, but it involves a great deal of unnecessary labour. And if the memory fails during the course of the lecture the effect might well be disastrous.

(3) *The extemporaneous method.* Here the *material* is carefully prepared beforehand in the sense that the lecturer knows exactly what facts he is going to use, and the order he will adopt in using them. The actual *language* in which the facts are stated comes naturally and fluently as the lecture proceeds. This method, which is undoubtedly the best, does not preclude the use of notes.

There are combinations of these three methods which need hardly engage our attention, except to point out that a lecturer who uses the extemporaneous method will find it necessary to memorize his outline if he does not use notes.

It is a common complaint amongst those who are new to the work of instructing or lecturing that although they know what they want to say yet they do not know how to introduce their subject. The importance of a good introduction is generally recognized. An audience can be roused to rapt attention or made completely indifferent in the first minute. If in that time a speaker can manage to impress his hearers he will probably be followed to the end. But if in that time he does not impress them he must continue under a serious handicap.

Every instructor must begin by adjusting himself to his squad or class, for the instructor who is vain enough to imagine that he can adjust other people to himself is doomed to failure. He must make the best of whatever presence he has. He must not adopt a slovenly attitude, but *stand* alert and erect. A man who is standing has a psychological advantage over others who are sitting. What the instructor has to say must *seem* important even before he begins to say it. The instruction begins immediately a speaker takes up his position, and before ever he opens his mouth. And when he does open his mouth, every word must be heard without the slightest strain being imposed on the listener. Persons who have to strain in order to catch what is being said very soon grow weary and cease to give attention.

An opening sentence ought never to be commonplace. If an instructor begins by saying: "I am going to talk this morning about the composition of an army," then he must not complain if the class assumes an attitude of repose. A commonplace opening suggests that the whole subject is commonplace, whilst an arresting opening suggests that the whole subject is arresting. To a class of gunners, for instance, the instructor might begin: "We all know that the Royal Regiment of Artillery is the biggest and best in the whole army. But there *are* other regiments; and this morning we are going to discuss how an army on active service is built up, what it consists of besides artillery, and what the other branches of the service do when the battle is joined."

In this instance the class is brought into the lecture with the first word—*we*. So it is going to be their lecture as well as the lecturer's? Good. Immediately they are given a personal reason for listening. Next, the lecturer makes a statement with which they are proud to concur: "*Our* regiment is the biggest and best in the whole army." He is a man of very sound sense, they feel, and well worth listening to. Go on!

A lecturer ought never to open with a sentence that creates doubt or provokes annoyance. He should begin with a statement that, without being commonplace, will find ready acceptance. If an audience is able to accept wholeheartedly the first three or four statements which a speaker makes, then the chances are it will accept all the others.

In regard to the actual delivery of a lecture there are certain points of psychological interest and value:

(1) A lecturer must never try to impress a class with his own cleverness. Other people are chiefly interested in *their* own cleverness, and if anything tends to give them a feeling of inferiority they will usually try to justify themselves by mentally challenging what they are told.

(2) He should always *state* his points, and never *argue* them. An argumentative style is apt to arouse in others a feeling of hostility.

(3) The most important personal element in making a talk interesting is one's own enthusiasm for the subject. Enthusiasm—like measles—is catching.

(4) If questions are asked, the same two or three persons should not be allowed to make all the answers. In a discussion an endeavour should be made to get everyone to say something.

(5) A question must never be framed in this form: "Snooks, how many battalions are there in an infantry brigade?" If it is, Sniffkins, O'Grady and company, will not bother to find the answer. Rather should it ask, "How many battalions are there in an infantry brigade—Private Snooks?" No name should be mentioned till the whole class has mentally responded.

(6) A lecturer should not walk about while speaking. If he does the class will concentrate its attention on his movements rather than on his words.

If an instructor has prepared his subject well—and he has no business to be instructing if he has not—then whatever notes he has with him should be of the scantiest. A constant reference to notes, except for technical details, etc., detracts from the force of delivery. Anyone who aims at being a really first-rate instructor or lecturer will take pains to rely less and less upon notes till he is able to dispense with them altogether.

Hardly less important than the introduction of a lecture is the conclusion, for if that is good the class will more readily take away the impression that the whole was good. Here it is generally a wise plan for the lecturer to recapitulate very briefly the points that have been brought out without wearying the class with unnecessary repetitions. He should never conclude with some indeterminate phrase, such as: "Well, there you are, and that's about all there is to it," but finish with a telling sentence that is likely to be remembered.

It is recorded that when old Samuel Rogers told a story that failed to produce a laugh he would observe in a reflective tone: "The curious part of that story is that stupid people never see the point of it." This device never failed to stimulate loud, though belated, guffaws.

A good instructor will aim at giving his class the impression that they have been clever enough to grasp every point that was made; and in the event of a discussion it is wise to let them believe that they have discovered the truth for themselves. There are tricks in every trade, and by far the most difficult and important trick in the trade of a speaker is to be completely self-effacing. An audience should be conscious of what is being said rather than of the person who says it. It should believe that the ideas are its own rather than the speaker's. And it should be allowed to take to itself the credit for what it has grasped.

Leadership is indeed a way of life.

CHAPTER SIX

EXAMPLE

When a man joins one of the services he feels like a fish out of water. Everything is new to him. Probably for the first time since he was born he finds himself in a world of strangers. The sooner he is made to feel at home the sooner he will settle down to serious training. It seems to be taken for granted that a man cannot really be happy in the services, and that the best that can be done is to make life bearable. The good leader will make it his business to keep the members of his group not only contented but *happy*. The second best is just not good enough.

When an officer or non-commissioned officer takes over a new group of men he will go a long way towards creating a good impression, and winning their confidence, if he observes certain common-sense rules. A group is likely to keep its first impression of its leader even though the impression be false. Therefore it is a sound plan to turn the tables and begin by giving the group something to do. Before addressing a word of introductory speech to the men he should give them five minutes' energetic drill. This will impress them with the fact that he means business and is to be obeyed. Moreover, he has gained the initial psychological advantage of having placed himself in the position of one who is forming a judgment of his men, instead of his men forming a judgment of him.

This matter having been satisfactorily settled the group may take its ease while the leader introduces himself in words that ought not to occupy more than three minutes. He should make quite sure beforehand that they have been told his name. His identity is thus established. He is an individual. He should go out of his way to be friendly and create a good impression. Why not?

If he can raise a laugh so much the better, but it must not be at someone's expense. He should tell his men that he is going to back them up, and ask them to back him up by "jumping to it," and by being clean, and smart and soldierly. The leader wants the best section, or platoon or company in the regiment. It is in the interest and power of his men to give it him, and give it him they certainly will if he goes to the trouble of handling them properly. The men themselves want to belong to the best platoon in the company, and to the best company in the battalion. The average decent and well-brought up Englishman has no wish to "dodge the column." When troops begin to shirk there is something wrong with the leadership.

The men who compose a badly-run group will very soon reflect in their own characters all the vices which they see around them. To take this "dodging the column" business: we are sometimes told that the British soldier's greatest weakness is the fact that he is casual, and that if he can "dodge the column" he will do so. This is sheer nonsense. The Empire cannot have been built up by shirkers. For hundreds of years the British soldier has proved that he is without an equal. Again and again he has taken on his opponents at odds of three to one, and found himself at no disadvantage. No doubt he has his weaknesses, but these are more often due to faulty organization and indifferent leadership.

"Hanging about" is the curse of the British army. Far too much time is allowed for everything. We are training men for battles that will be fought out at incredible speed, when every single minute will be precious, and yet we loiter around as if time was the least important thing in life. The psychological effect of this is simply disastrous. To take one instance—the weekly pay parade. In the average unit it drags on for at least an hour, and in some cases very much longer. It starts with *Abbot* and goes right through the alphabet till it concludes with *Yule*; but *Yule* is made to parade at the same time as *Abbot*. In the winter he freezes in the cold, and in the summer he fries in the heat—and is expected to like it. It is the height of madness to punish men for not being keen and alert if they are living under a system that encourages procrastination and idleness.

In the Royal Navy a ship's company of twelve hundred officers and men can parade punctually on the hour, and be dismissed to their respective duties in less than three minutes. The standard of cleanliness which the navy demands of its personnel is not lower than that of the army.

Unpunctuality on the part of a subordinate rank is quite properly treated as a crime. In a superior it is an infinitely more serious failing, not only because of the great inconvenience and exasperation it causes, but because it is damaging to efficiency and destructive of morale.

If troops are to be made keen and alert then everything from reveille to last-post must go like clockwork. There must be no hanging about. Strict punctuality must be demanded of all ranks. Officers and non-commissioned officers must set an example. It is the duty and privilege of leaders to—lead.

Before an officer or non-commissioned officer can be a successful leader his subordinates must have confidence in him (*a*) as a man, and (*b*) as a soldier. They will judge him as a man by his character and personality; and as a soldier by his appearance and ability. Does he want his men to be the best turned-out in the regiment? Then he must set them an example. His ambition is much more likely to be realized if his own turn-out is faultless. If he wants his men to "jump to it" then he must develop a word of command that is incisive and compelling. If he wants to ensure a loyal attitude towards himself then he must go out of his way to be loyal alike to his subordinates and superiors. If he wants to have the most efficient group in his unit then he had better take care to be the most efficient leader in his unit. Like breeds like. Men will mould themselves according to the pattern of a leader whom they respect. It is not sufficiently realized that they are proud, and even boastful, of an efficient leader, for they share in his glory.

The group must be regarded as a team, and the leader as the captain of the team. The captain of a team does not stand on the touchline roaring criticism and advice. He gets into the thick of the game, encouraging his men by his own enthusiasm and example. If the occasion demands it, then officers and non-commissioned officers should never hesitate to take off their tunics, roll up their sleeves and join actively in the job. The psychological effect of such complete identity of purpose is staggering.

The members of the team from the Commanding Officer downwards should know each other thoroughly. Only too often the Commanding Officer is regarded by his men as a species of stipendiary magistrate whose unaccustomed proximity bodes ill for all parties, but especially for the troops, and whose chief occupation would appear to be the committing of malefactors to the *glass-house*. How can morale be cultivated under conditions such as these?

It is essential that troops should see their Commanding Officer constantly when they are in training taking an absorbing interest in the progress of their work. It would be a sound practice if once a week at least he drilled each company in his battalion, and even smaller formations at times. Needless to say these occasions should be quite informal and impromptu, otherwise inefficient Company Commanders will have their men "spitting and polishing" for days beforehand, and what ought to be an interesting, and even inspiring, interlude in their training will be looked forward to with loathing and dread.

The Company Commander should drill each platoon as often as possible. The Platoon Commander should drill each section. And these junior officers should be given the opportunity of drilling other and larger formations than their own. By such methods they would gain confidence in their own powers of command; and the complete unit would become familiar with its leaders. A spirit of comradeship and confidence would be born that would prove unconquerable in the day of battle. Men are much more likely to back up leaders they know than leaders whom they only half know.

The officer who is an athlete will, of course, represent his group in whatever sport he excels. The psychological effect of his presence on the field is in itself a valuable contribution to his side. If he is not an athlete then he had better busy himself in some form of activity connected with games. If he can referee a game let him do so. Every officer and non-commissioned officer who can be spared from duty should be on the touchline during an important match. If the leaders show themselves to be men of energy and enthusiasm, with a burning interest in all the affairs of the group, their subordinates will follow them blindly through fire and water.

CHAPTER SEVEN

WHAT'S IN A NAME?

It is recorded that when Disraeli was accosted by anyone who claimed acquaintance, but whose name and face he had forgotten, he used always to enquire in a tone of affectionate solicitude, "And how is the old complaint?"

Disraeli was a very wise man. He knew that human beings like to talk about themselves and to be made to feel important. But more than that: he had learned that one of the greatest indignities we can inflict upon our fellow-man is to let him know we have forgotten his name. For we have let him see that we do not regard him as a person of the slightest consequence.

Anyone who aspires to be a successful leader must exploit to the full whatever qualities of character and personality and intelligence he possesses. It is an idle excuse for a man to claim, "I can't remember names." A leader must make it his *business* to remember names. We do not forget our own names or the names of our friends. If we did we would be given a ticket and clapped in a home. To tell the truth we do not easily forget anyone's name if we regard him as a person of importance.

A leader must regard each separate member of his group as of the *greatest* importance. Dale Carnegie, who knows more about applying psychology to human relations than any other man, says this: "A man's name is to him the most important thing in the English language."

Dale Carnegie has a refreshing habit of talking very good sense.

"*A man's name is to him the most important thing in the English language.*"

That is one of the first lessons to be learnt by anyone who aspires to win the confidence of his fellow-men.

THE army leader of modern times who was most idolized by his troops was the late Field-Marshal Lord Roberts. He was said to possess an uncanny gift of remembering names. What was his method? He would ride up behind a column of troops on the march and quietly ask an officer in the rear:

"What Company is this?"

" '*D*' *Company, sir.*"

"What is the name of that man who is limping?"

"*Snooks, sir.*"

"And the lance-corporal next to Snooks?"

"*Sniffkins, sir.*"

"And the man immediately in front of Snooks?"

"*O'Grady, sir.*"

With this information duly registered in his mind Lord Roberts would then ride ahead:

"Hullo, so it's Private Snooks! Are your poor old feet troubling you? I'm so sorry. You've stuck it out magnificently, Private Snooks. That's grand. Keep going, my fine fellow, keep going. Platoon Commander: see that Private Snooks gets every attention at the first available opportunity. We must have him fit again as soon as possible.

"So *you're* there, Lance-Corporal Sniffkins! It's very gallant of you to carry Private Snooks' rifle. That's the spirit I like to see in a non-commissioned officer. Thank you, Corporal, thank you.

"What! Private O'Grady here, too? How much service have you now? Eighteen months! Why, you're stepping it out like a veteran. You're as smart a young soldier as ever I set eyes on. Next time you write home tell them what I said about you. You'll be a credit to your regiment one day, Private O'Grady.

"Well done, 'D' *Company*. I'm proud of every man amongst you. Show the enemy your mettle when we catch up with him. Lace him, 'D' *Company*. Shoot straight. Let him see what British troops are made of. Carry on, 'D' *Company*. Carry on!"

Do we need to be told that "*D*" *Company* was good for another ten miles, and quite undaunted by odds of five to one?

It might be asked, "Did not the methods of Lord Roberts amount to sheer humbug?" Most certainly they did not. No man that ever lived was more proud of his soldierly profession, nor had a deeper and more lasting affection for those who served under him. He was wise enough to realize the vast importance of being able to call a man by his own name; and in taking the trouble to find out the man's name beforehand he was perfectly sincere. He asked because he really wanted to know. And having been told a name he remembered it, not because he had a good memory, but because he had a big heart.

When we call a man by his name we give him an identity. He is no longer a man in the crowd, but an individual. We have given him a sense of importance and a feeling of confidence and respect.

To be able to remember names is not a gift, and to forget names is not an indication of a weak memory. When we have a strong personal interest in a man we have little difficulty in remembering his name.

Most people can remember about five hundred names, but with a little training and method the mind is able to cope with considerably more. A good plan is to write down in a special notebook a list of ten names, in the first place, devoting a page to each name. All the details by which it is possible to identify each person should be added: his job, rank, appearance, home town, etc. When a name has been learnt no opportunity should be lost of accosting that particular individual, and addressing him by name.

In conversation he should be encouraged to talk about himself: he should be asked about his family, his home, and his job. All relevant information should go down in the notebook, and it must be constantly checked. He will soon begin to realize that he is regarded as a person of interest and importance. That is a good thing for him, and it is a good thing for his leaders.

When ten names have been completely mastered attention should be given to an additional ten. By constant reference to the notebook it is possible to ascertain progress.

The effect which a senior officer can produce by stopping a private soldier and addressing him by name is electrical. Needless to say, no one should ever be asked his name if it is possible to learn it in any other way. If a man's name is momentarily forgotten care should be taken to conceal the fact from him.

Not only ought troops to know the names of all the officers in the regiment, but in addition they should know those of their Brigadier, Divisional Commander, Corps Commander, and Army Commander, together with all facts concerning these senior officers that are of interest and importance: the regiments in which they served, the appointments thay have held, their decorations, etc. All this helps to build up *esprit de corps* and is an aid to good morale. Troops cannot be expected to have confidence in a Divisional Commander, for instance, if they do not even know his name. Until they do know his name, and a great deal about him, he might just as well not exist so far as they are concerned.

It used to be a custom in the army—and a very good custom too—never to address a non-commissioned officer or a private soldier without mentioning his rank. Lance-Corporal Sniffkins has a right to be called *Lance-Corporal Sniffkins* on all occasions, and not merely when he is on parade. Private Snooks feels proud when he is called *Private Snooks*. Why not let him feel proud? If he is given a feeling of dignity he will try to live up to it.

Subordinates should be discouraged from referring to their superiors by initials. A General Officer Commanding-in-Chief is the *Commander-in-Chief* and not the *C.-in-C.* The Commanding Officer of a regiment ought not to allow himself to be referred to by every Tom, Dick and Harry as the *C.O.* Warrant officers and non-commissioned officers should not be referred to by letters as if they were brands of sauce. No one should be so ill-mannered as to call a medical officer *Doc*. And no one could blame the dental officer for being revenged on a patient who had ever called him—*Toothy!*

Is there any wonder that the English are considered to

possess a remarkable aptitude for the gentle art of making enemies? It never pays to make a man feel humiliated or unimportant, even though the slight be unintentional.

But above all:

"A man's name is to him the most important thing in the English language."

CHAPTER EIGHT

THE PSYCHOLOGY OF LEADERSHIP

Dealing with human nature is the biggest problem a leader has to face. This is true not only of military leaders but of all who hold positions of authority over their fellow men. A great industrialist, for instance, does not outstrip his competitors because his knowledge of manufacturing processes is greater than theirs, but because of his ability to obtain from his staff an uncommonly high percentage of efficiency. The most learned man does not necessarily make the best teacher. The cleverest doctor does not always have the largest practice. The most accomplished player in the side is not necessarily the best captain. In a leader the ability to arouse enthusiasm, and to weld a number of individuals into a team, is of far greater importance than knowledge and skill.

Nor should this fact discourage those who have taken the trouble to equip themselves with knowledge and skill. True, it is often their experience to be outstripped in their careers by rivals whom they regard as their intellectual inferiors. But where there is knowledge and skill, plus the ability to arouse enthusiasm, there we have a Nelson or a Napoleon, a Cromwell or a Churchill.

An instance of the art of arousing enthusiasm has been

given in the case of Lord Roberts. The value of this art will be appreciated even more highly if we compare the incident that has been described with a somewhat exaggerated picture of what might have happened if Lord Roberts had belonged to the "Put-the-fear-of-God-in-them" school. He rides up behind the column and asks Snooks what the *so-and-so* he means by hopping about the road in that fashion, and curses him for a weakling and a malingerer. He calls Sniffkins a *something* fool for carrying Snooks' rifle and orders him to return it. He tells O'Grady he is a duck-footed son of a *what-do-you-call-it*, and threatens him with the guard-room if he does not step it out. And after telling the company in general that they are a disreputable mob of *so-and-so's* and a disgrace to the British army, he rides ahead in order to "put some guts" into the other companies.

Three hours later *"D" Company* goes into action. The personnel are just the same. But their morale is gone. Now they have no confidence in themselves, and certainly they have none in their supreme leader. They have lost the battle before a shot has been fired, and can easily be routed by a force vastly inferior in numbers, training and equipment.

When Napoleon laid it down that "Moral force to the physical is as three to one," he erred on the side of understatement. Psychologists are now generally agreed that the average man uses only ten per cent of his physical and mental resources.

The difference between the amount he uses and that at his disposal is also the difference between what he is now and what he might be.

A good leader is one who can persuade, or inspire, his subordinates to contribute more than ten per cent of their physical and mental resources; and a bad leader is one who has the effect of making them contribute less. When it is considered that the moral force of an army of one hundred thousand men is incalculably greater than the sum total of the moral force of the one hundred thousand individuals who make up that army, it will be appreciated how vastly important is the whole subject.

The primary duty of a leader, then, is to arouse enthusiasm in (*a*) the individual members of the group, and (*b*) the group as a team. In the past we have concentrated on the latter of these two points to the neglect of the former. Are we to be content with only ten per cent of an individual's fighting power and efficiency when the individual himself is desperately anxious to contribute one hundred per cent?

"Weapons change," says Henderson, "but human nature —which is the paramount consideration of all questions of either tactics or strategy—remains unaltered." In dealing with individuals it is well to remember that there is only one way to develop the best in any man, no matter what his rank or station, and that is by encouragement. There never was an outstanding leader who did not bear that fact constantly in mind. "The deepest principle in human nature," says a famous psychologist, "is the craving to be appreciated." Criticism may relieve the feelings of the critic, but no matter how justified it may be it can arouse only resentment or discouragement in the person who is criticized. Appreciation, on the other hand, stirs a man to give of his best.

There used to be a wise and experienced Commanding Officer serving a number of years ago who, finding himself impressed by the beauty and tidiness of a soldier's garden, always took particular care to say so. Immediately the man's eyes would light up with pride and enthusiasm. Henceforth it was almost impossible for that man to neglect his garden, for he was anxious to retain not only the Colonel's good opinion, but also the good opinion which he had instinctively formed of himself. Invariably he would set himself an even higher standard, and his enthusiasm was often so infectious that he rarely failed to spur on his neighbours to rival him. In the final result the appearance of a whole block of married quarters would change for the better, and the individuals concerned were in every way a great deal more friendly and happy.

If this Commanding Officer thought he required advice about his own garden he found it a profitable plan to go out of his way to consult a soldier who had made no great success of his army career, and who was probably suffering from feelings of inferiority and frustration in consequence. "I am having trouble with *so-and-so*," he would say. "What do you advise me to do?"

The effect he produced was invariably startling, for in a moment the man would be transformed into a figure of animation and eagerness. Would not the Colonel come in while the matter was explained? Look, what did he think of those tomatoes and would he please take a pound or so? "Missis, get a paper bag." He forced upon his Colonel the best stuff he had in his garden, and he would have been deeply hurt had it been refused.

What had happened? Simply this.

Snooks, who had never counted for very much, and had been constantly reminded of his many failings and delinquencies, suddenly learnt that his own Commanding Officer respected him as an authority on gardening. Possibly for the first time in his life he had been given a feeling of real importance. No matter how dull-witted Snooks may be his craving to be appreciated is not less than that of a more able man. Indeed, it is probably far greater. And whoever takes the trouble to gratify that craving will be rewarded to the limit of Snooks' ability. His humble ten per cent may appear small beside the ten per cent of other men, but his one hundred per cent may be four or five times greater than the ten per cent of really able men. There is no man so dull that he has not some talent that can be praised. Whoever takes the trouble to praise it is generally rewarded with rich and constantly recurring dividends.

A Commanding Officer should lose no opportunity of expressing his appreciation of any outstanding work on the part of a subordinate officer. The subordinate officers, warrant officers and non-commissioned officers must in turn go out of their way to praise good work on the part of the troops. Criticism there must be at times, but it should always aim at being constructive, and it ought never to be destructive.

If morale is to be raised, and maintained at a high level, then the officer or non-commissioned officer of fretful temperament, who has a tendency to nag, should be quietly corrected. Some individuals have nagging voices. They should be asked to change them. A leader will get the best value out of his subordinates if he takes the trouble to treat them with patience, courtesy and consideration.

In every company or battery there will be half a dozen men who are awkward or unpopular. Often they are the butt of their own comrades, besides being the unhappy victims of a great deal of coarse abuse from a certain unsatisfactory type of non-commissioned officer. It is by no means beyond the power of a really good leader to convert some of these men into loyal and hard-working troops. It will usually be found that thay have spent the greater part of their lives absorbing kicks and cuffs they were not quick enough to dodge. They must be given a sense of dignity. They should be encouraged to take up something at which they are likely to succeed: to ride one of the company push-bikes; to excel at something, no matter what—running, gymnastics, or even darts; to drive a vehicle if they can be trusted so far; and the leader should be lavish in expressing his appreciation of any good work they do. This appreciation must be quite sincere. Above all, the King's Commission ought never to be compromised—apart from the character of an officer and gentleman—by cheap jokes at their expense. There are many mean forms of humour, but that surely is the meanest. All attempts to keep them at a disadvantage should be sternly suppressed.

It is not pretended that a leader will not have occasion every day to reprimand the conduct or to criticize the work of a subordinate. There is a right way and a wrong way of doing that. It is the duty of a leader to inculcate in his subordinates specific habits of success. How will he best do that? By encouragement or discouragement? By giving a man a high standard to live up to, or by exposing him as a fool? When a man has to be criticized it is wise first of all to remind him that he has fallen below his own standard. He can be spurred on to greater efforts by a spirit of approval, but he can only develop feelings of inferiority under a spirit of destructive criticism.

The question will inevitably be asked by some: Are fighting troops to be treated as if they were a lot of old women? It will suffice to say for the present that the methods which are advocated here have been practised by every great leader—and they have worked. A study of biography will soon verify that. Lesser men have lacked the initiative, or common sense, to exploit these methods with regrettable consequences to themselves and their subordinates. Anyone who feels the slightest doubt about them has only to give them an honest trial for a single day. They will produce results that speak for themselves.

CHAPTER NINE

CARE OF MEN

Courage and discipline alone will not help an army to victory unless it can fight better than the enemy. The constant anxiety of every commander in the field is the amount of fighting-power that will be available to him at any particular place, and at any particular time. "The end of strategy is the pitched battle," says Henderson, "and it is hardly necessary to point out that the encounter at which the strategist aims is one in which every possible advantage of numbers, ground, supplies, and morale shall be secured to himself, and which shall end in his enemy's annihilation."

Fighting is the real end to be kept in view in any system of training. No army can stand up against the speed and dash of modern war unless it possesses great powers of endurance. What is it that causes the long casualty rolls during a campaign? Not the losses in actual battle, but the steady, never-ceasing disease brought about by insufficient and badly-cooked food, ceaseless toil, night duties, lack of sleep, and by exposure to extremes of heat and cold. "Swords and lances," says an American medical specialist, "arrows, machine guns, and even high explosives have had far less power over the fates of the nations than the typhus louse, the plague flea, and the yellow fever mosquito."

To quote an official training memorandum: "Care of men is a necessary foundation of all successful training." Without human beings there can be no fighting at all. Without human beings who are physically fit there can be no sustained fighting under modern conditions. And without human beings who are psychologically fit and possess the will to win there can be no decisive victory. War begins and ends, not with dive-bombers and tanks, not with equipment and supplies, not with maps and terrain, but with human beings.

In *Generals and Generalship* Field-Marshal Lord Wavell quotes a passage that is attributed to Socrates:

"The general must know how to get the men their rations, and every other kind of stores needed for war. He must have imagination to originate plans, and practical sense and energy to carry them through. He must be observant, untiring, shrewd; kindly and cruel; simple and crafty; a watchman and a robber; lavish and miserly; generous and stingy; rash and conservative. All these and many other qualities, natural and acquired, he must have. He should also, as a matter of course, know his tactics; for a disorderly mob is no more an army than a heap of building materials is a house."

And General Wavell comments on this passage: "Now the first thing that attracts me about that definition is the order in which it is arranged." In short, it begins with human beings, and not with strategy or tactics.

A great deal is written in this book about the importance of officers and non-commissioned officers knowing their men. That is the first thing necessary to good leadership. But it is by no means the only thing. Knowing a man is but the first step towards winning his confidence and respect. A leader must know his men in the sense that he knows their mental make-up, their thoughts and moods, their grouses and worries, their family circumstances, their past history and future ambitions; he must know all these things as one who is genuinely interested. He should therefore endeavour to be accessible to his men as much as possible.

Every officer should make it his business to acquire a stout and serviceable note-book which he should regard as his personal *Pocket Book*. It must not be used for items of passing interest, but only for information of permanent value. With his *Pocket Book* in front of him he should study carefully the many *Army Training Memoranda*, and copy out those paragraphs that can be put to practical use: care of men; health of troops; discipline and punishments; morale; dress; saluting; drill and physical fitness, etc. These are some of the items that have been dealt with by experts. By copying out the more important points an officer can thus make them belong to him; and by constantly adding to them as a result of wider reading as well as by his own every-day experience, he will soon possess an excellent working manual of his own.

With his own manual as a practical guide he can then proceed to order his military life and duties in the light of his own precepts. It is only by giving attention to the little extra things that anyone can ever become an outstanding leader. It is the very important duty of even the most junior commander to back up his Commander-in-Chief by putting into the field every possible man, fighting fit and determined to win, and every single piece of equipment that will help to ensure success.

That is so very important that it is necessary to repeat it; and it ought to figure prominently in the *Pocket Book:*

It is the duty of even the most junior commander to back up his Commander-in-Chief by putting into the field every possible man, fighting fit and determined to win, and every single piece of equipment that will help to ensure success.

This duty begins long before the battle-field is ever in sight. Indeed it begins immediately the recruit joins the army. A good officer will see to the comfort and welfare of his men at all times. If his troops are in camp or in billets he should make it his personal responsibility to ensure that their living quarters are weatherproof. He should take care to see that each of his barrack-rooms possesses its dart-board and wireless set. These can often be obtained from the Comforts Fund of newspapers, women's associations, etc. Usually the Chaplain is able to tap sources of supply which are unknown to the ordinary layman.

On active service, too, it is more important than ever that troops should be as comfortable as circumstances will permit when they are not in action. In *Scouting for Boys*, that wise old campaigner, the late Lord Baden-Powell, accumulated a wealth of useful information for those who, from necessity or choice, live in the open. This book is as good a half crown's worth as could be found anywhere. A great deal of the information contained in it can be imparted to troops in those odd periods of ten and fifteen minutes which are available for instructional purposes.

A good officer must ever be on the look-out for new tips. No opportunity should be lost of inspecting living conditions in units other than one's own, for these conditions vary tremendously even in peace time. By careful arrangement many units are able to purchase table equipment and decorations, and their dining-rooms are so spotlessly clean and well kept that they are vastly superior to many first-class restaurants.

On active service particular care should be taken to ensure that as far as possible there is no falling off in the standard of feeding. It is well known that during the last war troops were commonly more vigorous in attack after a good hot breakfast than they were after an indifferent meal.

The health of troops is the concern not only of the medical officer. "Prevention is better than cure." If a man is constantly reporting sick then quite definitely there is something wrong with either his body or mind. Possibly it is his mind. It is not a doctor he wants so much as an audience. He has a subconscious desire to talk about his troubles. There is no harm in that, and he should be encouraged to do so.

A unit of keen troops will generally have a small sick parade. Certainly no man ought ever to be discouraged from reporting sick, but it remains a fact that persons who are happy and keen about their work are more generally healthy than the mentally, morally or spiritually fed-up.

Every officer should be able to render first aid. There are many excellent text books of a compact size which can easily be carried in a battle-dress pocket when on active service. The officer who can do the little extra things, in addition to the normal things, is likely to exert most influence.

During training hours an officer ought not to be slacking in the company office when his men are marched off to the gymnasium for physical training. He should go with them, both with the object of satisfying himself that they are making good progress, and also because they will appreciate the personal interest he is taking in their work.

If he is a hero he will sometimes fall in with the class and "go through the hoop" with them. This is not courting popularity. It is his duty to identify himself as much as possible with his group. An officer who takes this kind of interest need never bother himself about problems of leadership, for he has solved them all. His men will follow him instinctively. Needless to say, the physical training staff should be warned when an officer is joining the class, otherwise he runs the risk of having certain offensive remarks directed at those portions of his anatomy which protrude.

The regimental canteen, and other institutes where men forgather during off-duty hours, should be visited regularly. It is often said that troops do not want to see their officers during off-duty hours. That depends entirely on the officers. It is the duty of an officer to satisfy himself that his men are being properly looked after by those organizations which are authorized to provide for the social and moral welfare of the army.

Lord Roberts always set tremendous value on the duty of visiting his men in hospital, and even when he occupied positions of supreme command he took every opportunity of cheering the sick. Throughout the whole of his service he could never hear unmoved of any man being killed or wounded; and many a home in the British Empire, from the highest to the humblest, had cause to remember him gratefully for the letters or telegrams he sent when wives or parents were racked with anxiety. In this regard every officer would do well to emulate him. Troops are very human, and like to feel that they are appreciated as individuals and not merely as fighting machines.

If detention barracks are within reasonable distance it is a sound practice to visit any unfortunate who is undergoing punishment. There must be no suggestion that he has disgraced the unit, nor must there be any lavish expressions of sympathy. He should be treated as a normal human being, and quietly encouraged with wise counsel to live down the past by trying to distinguish himself in the future. That is a line which often succeeds.

This chapter is not intended as a catalogue of *Hints for Young Officers*, but is meant to draw attention to the psychological value of those little extras which mark the difference between a good and a bad leader. Every conscientious officer should take care to adapt the precepts of his *Pocket Book* to the psychology of his own particular men. A leader will handle his group infinitely better when he has learnt to handle the vastly different individuals who make up the group.

CHAPTER TEN

TEAM SPIRIT

A number of years ago two Scottish regiments, that shall be nameless, were stationed at a certain camp in the Aldershot command. About fifty per cent of their personnel at that time were cockneys, for when the cockney is given a choice of regiments he usually chooses one that has its depot north of the border. His pride in the kilt is immeasurably greater than that of any highlander; and no human being ever experiences a rapture so intense as a cockney when he first hears himself called *Jock*.

But a kilt does not make a Scotsman any more than an

aptitude for profanity makes a bargee. Scotsmen are men who possess certain marked characteristics, and one of those is thrift. Each Friday evening pandemonium reigned in the vicinity of the camp post office, for every man and boy on the strength of those two regiments seemed to be there endeavouring to bank his pay. Even the cockneys were there. They liked to be taken for real Scotsmen, and they had wit enough to know that if they were to pass as real Scotsmen they must do as Scotsmen do. Consequently there was almost a riot at that post office every Friday evening.

But on Monday evening there *was* a riot. True, the crowd was only half the size of what Friday's had been, but it shoved, and jostled, and fought with a ferocity that made Friday's performance seem singularly well-behaved and lacking in enthusiasm. The explanation? On Monday the cockneys invariably returned to withdraw their money. A week-end of thrift was quite enough for them. Native habit had triumphed over team spirit, for at heart the cockney was a cockney still. The moral? Birds of a feather must flock together.

Most of the previous chapters have dealt with the subject of putting the leader in a position to lead his group. One of his chief duties is to develop and harness the collective mind of the group so that it can work with the maximum of power and effect. In other words he has to inspire in his men the team spirit. We use that term in preference to any other because the ordinary man knows at once exactly what it means. It means that each individual in the group feels that he is an essential part of a complete and self-contained unit—a body in which each member is expected to carry out his own individual part in order to attain the perfection and completeness of the whole.

The group, then, begins with the individual; and it must be realized that the team spirit can be built up only on the self-respect, self-control, self-confidence and self-discipline of individuals. It will thus be seen at once why it is so essential to treat each individual with courtesy, for instance. Such treatment gives him a sense of dignity; and a group of men with a sense of dignity will work harder, give less trouble, and fight better than a group of men with no sense of dignity at all.

If an individual is treated as a man of honour he will generally act as a man of honour. If he is treated as a man without honour, he is being invited to act as a man without honour. Each member of the group must be studied as an individual and treated as an individual. In a football team we recognize that a good centre-forward is not necessarily a good full-back. One man is good in attack, and another in defence. Care is taken to study the capability and temperament of each. And so it must be in an army if each individual is to put forth the best of which he is capable.

In training nothing must be taken for granted. Even drill will cease to be monotonous if men are told its real purpose. And so with other subjects. Every man understands that to defeat an enemy the first essential is to be able to fight better than he: to shoot straighter, to charge heavier, to march farther, to hang on longer, to work harder, to act quicker, and to stand steadier. Men need to be reminded again and again of the purpose and importance of each part of their training. If this is done it will cease to be a drudgery, and can even be made to infuse *esprit de corps*.

Doubtless a great deal more could be done for the individual through physical training. The Army Physical Training Staff is second to none in keenness and efficiency, and this is as it should be. Anyone who has watched a group of recruits come into barracks, and has followed their progress day by day for three months or so, must have been impressed by the miraculous transformation that has been effected: splay feet, round shoulders, pallid cheeks and distended paunches—these have quickly vanished under the magical power of the physical training instructor. Every man is proud of his body and his appearance. The one branch of training the average soldier looks forward to with enthusiasm is *P.T.* And yet it is the one branch of training in which the average officer displays least interest. A Company Commander makes it his personal business to follow the progress of his men in musketry; but often he does not look in the gymnasium from one month's end to another.

Recruits need little encouragement in regard to physical training, for it is taught by a specially selected and thoroughly trained staff; but its real purpose should be explained again and again. And further, it needs to be pointed out that it bestows benefits which remain with a man long after he has left the service. In addition to its more obvious physical advantages *P.T.* has equally important psychological advantages, for it inculcates self-respect, self-control, self-confidence and self-discipline.

In any large group of men joining the army there are individuals of every conceivable physical and psychological type: short and long, fat and thin, fair and dark, clean and dirty, alert and lazy, cheerful and sullen, honest and dishonest, virtuous and vicious, clever and stupid; and somehow these have to be welded together in one effective group. They start off with but few features in common, and the leader's task is to make their interests, loyalties, purposes and activities converge.

There must, then, be a standard, and whose standard is it to be? That of the clean, alert, cheerful, honest, virtuous and clever? Or that of the dirty, lazy, sullen, dishonest, vicious and stupid? If the matter is left to chance then the latter standard will undoubtedly prevail as every experienced non-commissioned officer knows. So it must *not* be left to chance. Indeed, the group standard to be aimed at should be far higher even than that of the best individuals.

Strangely enough even the most depraved and selfish

individual can often be inspired to do for the group what he could never be persuaded to do for himself. Everyone knows how a football fan who is normally shy and inoffensive will occasionally dress himself up in the most grotesque costume, and during the course of a game threaten with violence rival spectators who are twice his size because they have made remarks which reflect upon the skill of his own team. It is this extraordinary sentiment of group loyalty which an army must cultivate.

It would be a sound plan if every regiment and corps had its own handbook which could be sold to the recruit for a few pence: it could contain a brief history of the regiment, and dwell specially on those campaigns and battles in which the regiment fought with special distinction. Every man has a craving to be important, and for an individual who has never counted for very much in the whole of his life suddenly to find himself the heir and successor of a long line of heroes is a very gratifying experience. He will cheerfully work hard, under wise and considerate leadership, to acquire the moral qualities that have made his regiment famous: courage, endurance, obedience, trustworthiness, loyalty, etc. And under the influence of mass suggestion—for each member of the group is thinking along the same lines—he will come to despise laziness, dirtiness, cowardice, disobedience and disloyalty—indeed everything that detracts from the efficiency of his group.

Once the sentiment of group loyalty has been thoroughly aroused—and not before—it is possible successfully to influence each individual in regard to self-respect, self-control, self-confidence and self-discipline. The soldier can now be reminded how, since he entered the service, his very bearing and attitude have changed: he is alert, immaculate and full of vitality. In other words, physically he is as his Creator intended that he should be. But a soldier is something more than an individual with certain physical qualities.

He is also an individual with distinctive moral qualities. No profession can claim a longer line of unselfish and gallant service. And just as it is a fine thing to have a soldier's physical qualities, so it is a fine thing to possess a soldier's moral qualities.

Those qualities are self-sacrifice, loyalty, trust-worthiness, fair-play, honesty, obedience, discipline, courage, fortitude, cheerfulness, comradeship and kindness. These are the virtues which stamp an individual as a man of honour. And these are the virtues which have inspired individuals and regiments to fight with distinction and without counting the cost. Even in men who have been long hardened against every fine influence it is by no means impossible to infuse a desire for better things. It is notorious that men who are inured to a hard and dangerous life—and particularly soldiers and sailors—are commonly more courteous to women, more kind to children and animals, and more compassionate to the aged and infirm than other men. There is a psychological law of compensation by which hardness is balanced with tenderness, and sordidness with romance. And in the drudgery of training and the drabness of the camp men's minds are more eager to clutch at virtues which are bold and colourful.

This psychological urge needs to be scientifically exploited. Many a man in the services to-day is reading his Bible because it has been commended to him by the Empire's supreme authority—the King. And so men need to be encouraged by those whom they respect, and whose good opinion they value, to aim at the highest. By example, suggestion and group contagion everything should be done that can possibly be done to give each individual a set of ideals.

A man will commonly have more pride in his profession —and consequently in himself—if he understands its traditions. Every officer and non-commissioned officer would find it profitable to invest in *Military Origins*[1] by Brigadier C. T. Tomes. This excellent little book deals with such subjects as the national flag, regimental colours, saluting, duties on guard, ceremonial drill, military music, uniform and rank. Each chapter will furnish a ten minute talk of absorbing interest and will do much to arouse and foster the team spirit.

There are three qualities which have made the British Army in the past, and are no less important to it at the present time: discipline, team spirit, and power of endurance; and of these the greatest is undoubtedly team spirit. It is that which inspires a man to do so much more than his bare duty. And in order that this spirit may be sustained a man should never be transferred from one unit to another against his will except for the most imperative reasons, nor should he be moved even from one barrack-room to another unless it is absolutely necessary. Such moves are inimical to a healthy team spirit. Not only do they upset friendships, but no man cares to be messed about. Sometimes, of course, a change is desirable, particularly after a man's return from detention barracks, when a different environment might help him to make a fresh start. But in no circumstances ought a change to be made without the knowledge and authority of the Company Commander.

Team spirit depends on something more than a cap badge. In the first place the group must have some collective purpose. In the army the collective purpose of the small group—the platoon, company and battalion—is to demonstrate its superiority over similar groups. Every individual has a desire to belong to a group that excels and draws attention to itself, for the glory of such a group is reflected on the individuals who compose it. In every branch of training one group should work alongside another, and

[1] Published by Wm. Stevens, Ltd., York. One shilling (including postage).

they should be pitted against each other on every possible occasion. If one excels in the gymnasium the other should be encouraged to excel on the barrack-square. Competitions should be arranged to cover every form of activity, and enthusiasm should be maintained at the highest pitch. This can never be done by criticism, but only by encouragement.

The development of team spirit will depend more than anything upon the attitude and conduct of the officers. If they identify themselves completely with the group the team spirit will be strong, and if they fail to do so it will be weak. It is therefore imperative that the officers should get into the life of the group; into its activities, its barrack rooms and its games.

It is sheer nonsense to suggest that troops want to get away from their officers during off-duty hours. Those officers who make a practice of visiting barrack-rooms on certain evenings in the week very soon find that men who normally go out begin to stay in. At the first few visits some of the men are naturally shy, but they soon grow out of that. A good plan is for the officers of a company to take on a certain barrack-room at darts, the members of the other barrack-rooms in the company being allowed to attend as spectators. A game of rummy always goes down well and helps to keep the men from gambling. By methods such as these an intelligent officer very soon discovers exactly what is going on, and this is just as it should be. His influence should be as wide as possible.

It will be found in practice that the development of group loyalty in the platoon and in the company does not prevent, but rather facilitates, group loyalty in the regiment. This loyalty must find expression far beyond the regiment. Actually in war the division is the unit of organization, and a great deal can be done to inspire pride in the division. But the loyalty of each individual must stretch even beyond the division for it must take in the whole of the vast team that is captained by his supreme commander.

It must be the constant aim of all military leaders to develop the individual in both spirit and efficiency to be an effective member of the company. The company must be developed in spirit and efficiency to be an effective part of the regiment. The regiment, too, to be an effective part of the division. And the division to be an effective part of the army. In this way the moral force available to the Commander-in-Chief might well represent that very superiority which he needs in order to bring his campaign to a successful conclusion.

CHAPTER ELEVEN

MORALE: THE SECRET WEAPON

Morale is an army's secret weapon. Hitler sprang a secret weapon on us some time ago: the magnetic mine. But it was not so secret as he thought. True, it caused a great deal of damage and gave rise to much dismay so long as the secret remained a secret. In an incredibly short time, however, the Navy managed to pick up one and dissect it; and the secret was a secret no longer. A simple apparatus fitted to all our ships was sufficient to overcome the effect of one of the most devastating and ingenious of modern weapons.

Morale is not a secret in that sense, and it is not a weapon in that sense. Its existence has been known for thousands of years. But only the greatest leaders have been able to understand and exploit it. Napoleon seems to have known more about it than any other great military commander, and he said in effect that the man who was armed with it was worth three men who were not. Morale is a secret in the sense that it is invisible and intangible. It is the most powerful weapon known to men: more powerful than the heaviest tank; more powerful than the biggest gun; more powerful than the most devastating bomb. Again and again it has been the means of turning defeat into victory. An army is never beaten till it knows it is beaten, for defeat is an attitude of mind and not a physical condition.

To quote *Training Regulations*: "The development of morale is a vital object of training. Moral qualities include discipline, the fighting spirit, the will to win, self-control, self-respect, loyalty, and a high sense of honour."

It is not easy to find a satisfactory definition for such an imponderable quality as morale, but we shall not be misunderstood if we define it as *spiritual condition*. Morale is more than physical condition, and it is more than mental condition. It cannot fairly be restricted to moral condition. Indeed, it is something far greater than all of these together, and yet somehow grows out of them. In calling it *spiritual condition* we do not mean to imply that it is the prerogative of the religiously-disposed or the spiritually-minded. We use the definition in a philosophical, rather than a theological, sense; and if anyone dislikes it then he may substitute *psychological condition*, though it is less satisfactory.

Everyone is acquainted with the effects of a good morale. A football team in the third division will sometimes defeat a first-division side in a cup-tie in spite of the fact that so far as skill is concerned it is hopelessly outclassed. Here morale proves superior to skill. In the retreat from Mons in 1914 the comparatively small British force might well have been annihilated; but morale proved superior to numbers. The Germans were kept at bay not by fire-power—magnificent as that was in the circumstances—but by guts. Or to take the case of the German pocket-battleship *Graf Spee*: according to every physical calculation she ought to have shattered *Exeter, Ajax* and *Achilles* with her overwhelmingly superior gun-power. On the contrary she received such a plastering that she was compelled to cover her disgrace by committing *felo de se*. Again, the *Graf Spee* was beaten by guts. The British crews possessed vastly superior morale which more than made up for lack of gun-power. Had they not had superior morale they must inevitably have gone under.

The effects of a bad morale can be seen nowhere more vividly than in the tragic example of France. A nation which had been traditionally renowned for its *élan vital* found itself overthrown in a few weeks: its leaders in chains, its army in captivity, its granaries plundered, its press muzzled, its people—broken.

In his illuminating book, *Why France Fell*, Andre Maurois says: "Today one can say that the war was lost, so far as France was concerned, at the very moment it was begun." The Maginot line mentality—the leaving of all initiative to one's opponent—was bad enough in all conscience; but numerous other factors were even more insidious and dangerous. The physical condition of the army was bad owing to lack of modern equipment. Leadership was at a discount: for years it had been content to consult public opinion—instead of guiding it. Employers and workers regarded each other as natural enemies so that no united front could be formed against the arch-enemy. The nation's vitality was thus dissipated instead of being consolidated. Procrastination and lack of political method destroyed the ability to make decisions. These are largely moral factors, and they led to the disintegration of a first-class power.

Let us make no mistake, these same vices will disintegrate any group—a team, a regiment, or an army—if they are not rooted out. France fell because of (1) Bad leadership; (2) Lack of what we call *team spirit*; (3) Bad moral condition; (4) Lack of initiative and drive; and (5) Lack of discipline. Given time any one of these can lay civilization itself in the dust.

In passing it is of interest to glance at some of the remedies which M. Maurois proposes:

"*To be strong*. A nation that is not ready to die for its liberties will lose them.

"*To act quickly*. Ten thousand aeroplanes built in time are better than fifty thousand after the battle.

"*To direct opinion*. A leader shows the way; he does not follow.

"*To preserve a united country*. Political parties are passengers aboard the same ship; if they wreck it, all will perish.

"*To demand that those who govern lead upright lives*. Vice of any kind gives a foothold to the enemy.

"*To believe passionately in the ideas and in the way of life for which you are fighting*. It is faith that creates armies and even arms. Liberty deserves to be served with more passion than tyranny."

Brave words! They should be taken to heart by all who find themselves in the position of leaders.

All this goes to show that morale is a matter of life and death. It is not something we can afford to neglect. Every well-organized army is quite properly concerned in giving its troops a high standard of training and, if possible, weapons which will give them a physical superiority over their opponents. But physical superiority is not so important as moral superiority. An army had far better go into battle without ammunition than without morale.

How, then, can this most desirable of human qualities be acquired? It depends for its development, of course, on an incalculable number of factors: good leadership, discipline, professional training, equipment, a record of success, physical condition, mental condition, moral condition, patriotism, honour, self-respect, self-control, loyalty, the will to win, food, recreation, propaganda, etc.

But morale is not merely a state of conviction that is engendered by the cumulative effect of these factors, for the omission of one of them is often sufficient to negative all the others. In battle, bad leadership—for instance—may easily destroy morale though the other factors—training, equipment, past successes, etc.—are still there. It must be kept constantly in mind that when we deal with morale we deal with something that is not finite but infinite. Leadership is a way of life; and it inspires leader and led with a moral fervour which is the expression of a spiritual condition known as morale.

* * *

In the past the British army has been content to regard morale as the *moral effect* of the following:

> Training.
> Equipment.
> Physical condition (including food,
>   bodily comforts, etc.).
> Leadership.
> Discipline.
> *Esprit de corps.*

But if this supposition—and it is a very common one—were really true there would be normally little or no difference between the morale of two conflicting armies.

It would sometimes appear, indeed, as if this superficial estimate of morale were correct; but it will not bear close examination. In England's civil war between king and parliament, for instance, the forces of Charles I had every physical advantage: they were better trained and better equipped; they were in far better physical condition in that for the most part they were younger and more dashing; they were better led and—in a purely military sense—better disciplined; and they began with an infinitely higher standard of *esprit de corps*. Yet in the end they were thoroughly demoralized, hopelessly out-fought and overwhelmingly defeated. For when a struggle is prolonged, moral force—and not physical—will generally decide it.

That truth is so very important that it deserves to be repeated:

When a struggle is prolonged, moral force—and not physical —will generally decide it.

Charles I was really defeated by a moral fervour which his own cause lacked. An army of inspired amateurs wore down an army of gallant but uninspired professionals.

The ultimate object of every battle that is fought is psychological rather than physical. The real object is not necessarily to kill the enemy, or to cut him off from his resources, but rather to destroy his will to continue the fight. The present Nazi regime orders its strategy on the principle that it is much more economical to destroy wills than to destroy bodies. America discovered that wars are won by human beings. It was left to Germany to discover that wars are lost by human beings.

More than ever today armies are in need of morale. The morale which has been found adequate for training will not stand up for long periods against the violence of modern war: the dive-bomber with its screaming bombs, giant tanks belching out a murderous fire, and flamethrowers which scorch and demoralize. If men are to face such horrors and overcome them training and equipment in themselves are not enough.

There can be no proper morale where there is no self-confidence. A well-trained and well-equipped soldier will naturally feel morally, as well as physically, superior to an ill-trained and ill-equipped opponent, just as a well-dressed artisan feels morally superior to a labourer with a coloured handkerchief round his neck. Training, equipment, physical condition, leadership, discipline, *esprit de corps*—these must do everything they can to build up morale, and admittedly they can do a great deal. But yet a great deal more can be done.

The greatest handicap a man feels on joining the service is the loss of his personal liberty. He is forced to live to a time-table drawn up by somebody else. Even his evenings, when he might reasonably expect to feel at liberty, are often intruded upon by established authority. He is no longer free to dress as he pleases, or to go where he pleases. He can be ordered to do things against his will. His whole life is regulated without his wishes in the matter being consulted. His personality is merged in that of the group.

Needless to say, he cannot be expected to like all this, and it is wooden-headed to suggest that he should lump it.

In the first place care should be taken to ensure that his liberties are not encroached upon unnecessarily. The service demands of him strict punctuality, and he is reasonably entitled to expect that he will be rewarded with strict punctuality. Meals must be served to the minute, and adequate time allowed for their consumption. Saturday afternoons, and Sundays—after church parade—should be strictly observed as holidays: no unnecessary work should be carried out, nor should the troops be compelled to take a cross-country run, for instance, when they might reasonably want to do something else, or just to be left alone.

As far as possible evenings should be kept free of "spit and polish." If a man has done a good day's work then he has done as much as flesh and blood can reasonably be expected to do. Psychologists have exploded the asinine idea that if a man's nose is not kept to the grindstone during the whole of his waking hours he will inevitably come to a bad end. Men who work hard for a reasonable number of hours, and are then allowed a generous measure of liberty, will prove keener, happier, more efficient and better disciplined than those who are kept hard at it continually.

A watchful eye needs to be kept on the over-zealous non-commissioned officer who takes a delight in finding odd jobs that need to be carried out in off-duty hours. This type is a menace to morale.

As a form of psychological compensation for the loss of certain personal liberties the soldier should be encouraged to express his individuality in other directions. Games must not be the prerogative of the specialist; and if there is a shortage of grounds then the training programme should be arranged in such a way as to allow certain squads to play during the mornings instead of the afternoons.

Careful attention must be given to entertainments, and whenever possible the men should be encouraged to exploit their own talent.

The value of music in sustaining morale is generally recognized, but music can also play a large part in the building of morale. It breaks down personal barriers, and is a powerful means of merging individuals into a group. Officers should encourage all troops under their command who can play a mouth-organ to possess one. When they are played well they can do a great deal to brighten life in the barrack-room. Before route-marches, etc., a musical programme should be arranged for the road, and should be composed of rousing marching songs which the main body of troops can take up. Officers, warrant officers and non-commissioned officers should not regard it as beneath their dignity to take part in these musical outbursts. The psychological effect will be infinitely greater if all join in.

An American soldier, General J. F. Bell, has said: "A songless army would lack in fighting spirit in proportion as it lacked responsiveness to music. There is no more potent force for developing unity in an army than song."

And in support of this statement there is ample evidence. Hocking quotes at length a vivid passage from Frederick Coleman's *From Mons to Ypres*:

"Major Tom Bridges, of the 4th Dragoon Guards, had been sent into St. Quentin on Friday afternoon to see if more stragglers could be found. In the square near the Mairie he found a couple of hundred or more men of various detachments, who were seated on the pavement in complete exhaustion and utter resignation to what appeared their inability to rejoin the army which had retreated to the southward. Bridges needed but a moment to see how far gone they were, how utterly and hopelessly fatigued. No peremptory order, no gentle request, no cajolery would suffice. With most of them the power to move seemed to have gone with ceaseless tramping without food or sleep for the thirty-six hours past.

"A brilliant idea came to the big genial major. Entering a toy shop he bought a toy drum and a penny whistle. He strapped the little drum to his belt.

" 'Can you play *The British Grenadiers*?' he asked his trumpeter.

" 'Sure, sir,' was the reply.

"In a twinkling the pair were marching round the square, the high treble of the tiny toy whistle rising clear and shrill:

> *But of all the world's brave heroes*
> *There's none that can compare*
> *With a tow, row, row,*
> *To the British Grenadiers.*

"Round they came, the trumpeter, caught on the wings of the major's enthusiasm, putting his very heart and soul into every inspiring note. Bridges, supplying the comic relief with the small sticks in his big hands, banged away on the drum like mad.

"They reached the recumbent group. They passed its tired length. Now they came to the last man. Will they feel the spirit of the straining notes, rich with the tradition of the grand old air? Will they catch the spirit of the big-hearted major, who knows so well how the poor lads feel, and seeks that spot of humour in Tommy's make-up that has so often proved his very salvation?

"The spark has caught! Some with tears in their eyes, some with a roar of laughter, jump to their feet and fall in. Stiffened limbs answer to the call of newly-awakened wills. *With a tow, row, row, to the British Grenadiers.* They are singing it now, as they file in long column down the street after the big form hammering the toy drum, and his panting trumpeter.

"'Go on, Colonel. We'll follow you to hell,' sings out a brawny Irishman behind, who can just hobble along on his torn feet.

"Never a man of all the lot was left behind."

CHAPTER TWELVE

FEAR

Immediately a nation goes to war a set of fears is aroused in individuals—the fear of defeat, unsettlement, privation, loss of income, injury, etc. The man of military age who is called up, no matter how willingly and enthusiastically he responds, brings with him the fear of the unknown. Will he like the new life? Will his officers and non-commissioned officers treat him decently? Will his new comrades be of a congenial type? Will he be posted to the regiment or corps he wishes to join? How will his wife and children fare in his absence? And greatest fear of all: Will he survive? It needs to be realized by every single officer and non-commissioned officer that the fighting efficiency of an army depends chiefly upon the efficacy of the methods by which the instinct of fear is controlled.

If troops live in an atmosphere of uncertainty, if they are nagged, bullied and pursued, if methods of discipline are repressive rather than expressive, then indeed the fear instinct will be rampant and fighting efficiency will suffer. But if they are well looked-after and considerately treated, if they feel themselves to be bound together in one unconquerable team, there is simply no limit to the effort they can put forth.

It is the part of every leader to supplement in his subordinates that invincible courage which is the most miraculous attribute of human nature. For miraculous it is when it is considered how many fears there are to stifle it. That these fears can be excited, and native courage destroyed, by bad leadership is obvious to anyone who has thought seriously about the matter for five consecutive minutes.

Every individual, many times in life, experiences fear in varying forms and degrees, and the primitive instinct counsels concealment or flight. Usually the concealment takes the form of a lie. Flight may take various forms. It is not often that the victim of fear runs away in a physical sense, for if he did he would generally be compelled by circumstances to take the cause of his fear with him. Sometimes he seeks escape in intoxication or drugs. Or he deliberately shuts his eyes to his condition. If he is hopelessly in debt he spends the more. And more rarely his mind seeks an escape in insanity or suicide.

The natural antidote to fear is discipline. Indeed, discipline might almost be defined as the art of looking fear in the face. When it is bravely confronted it is never willing to do battle. It can inflict injury only when its victim is on the run. The individual who lives his life in accordance with a settled plan, who is a man of temperate habits and modest living, is much less likely to be haunted by the bogey of fear than the man who is content to live by the hour, who allows his life to drift and is unable to organize his work or leisure.

When obedience has become an instinct there is no chink in the armour through which fear can penetrate. When loading, taking aim, and firing have been done so often that their performance becomes automatic, then shooting wildly in the heat of the battle is not likely to occur. This kind of automatic efficiency in the individual gives him a sense of confidence.

And what is true in regard to the individual is not less true in regard to the group. For here drill is the means of imbuing a like confidence by synchronizing the action of each individual in such a way as to inspire a sense of solidarity. Each individual feels secure in the knowledge that every one of his comrades is at one with him, and not only constantly by his side and helping him, but at all times ready to come to his immediate aid. His identity is merged and his confidence strengthened in the group.

A badly-disciplined army will exhibit all the weaknesses and dangers which are common to every crowd, for it is discipline alone which converts a crowd into an army. Whereas a well-disciplined army is incapable of being intimidated by the sudden appearance of danger, a badly-disciplined army will react after the fashion of a mob, and disperse in a blind stampede. Just as in a well-disciplined army each individual's confidence is strengthened by that of his comrades, so in a badly-disciplined army each individual's instinct of fear is inflamed by the fear of those around him. Each one feels himself to be irresistibly driven to consult his own personal safety in immediate flight, and the cumulative influence is so terrible in its effect that no considerations of respect, decency or pity are allowed to stand in its way. Its victims often assume the irresponsible character of homicidal maniacs, and do not recover their balance till long after the danger has passed. In these circumstances it must seem incredible that persons are to be found who disparage the importance of discipline and drill.

Although discipline is a powerful element in combating fear there are many occasions in the field when it needs to be reinforced by other means. When troops are being subjected to intensive dive-bombing or artillery fire, for instance, and have to wait for some time before they are called upon to repel the main attack, it is advisable to divert their minds from present dangers by ordering some form of activity.

Messages can be passed up and down the line, rounds of ammunition can be polished and counted, there can be a little more digging in, rifles can be sighted at eight hundred yards, two hundred yards, five hundred yards—anything, indeed, that will help men to forget their fear. For even the bravest of men can feel afraid. The only difference between a brave man and a coward is that the fear of the one is controlled whilst the fear of the other is uncontrolled.

Here indeed is a great occasion for a wise leader whether his troops are waiting to attack or to be attacked. More than ever he has to inspire his men with the conviction that they are a group, that each man is supported by all the others, and that at the right moment the enemy is going to be "written off."

If there is time he should somehow endeavour to mention aloud each one of his men by name: "Well, Private Snooks, is the Bren ready to do its stuff? Good! Now, you're quite sure you've got your iron rations, Private Mulvaney? That's right. Plenty of water in that bottle, Private Bandolier? Sergeant, just help Private Foresight with his equipment."

Not only does this tend to give each individual a sense of respect and importance, but it is of inestimable value in letting each one see and feel that he enjoys the special interest and protection of the one man whom he wants at his side—and at whose side he wants to be.

It is also a good plan to encourage the men to carry out small services for each other. Not only does an individual commonly forget his own fear when he is called upon to help someone else, but the individuals concerned feel themselves as one.

Every leader must beware of the temptation to belittle the enemy's worth. In *Mein Kampf* Hitler confesses to the rude shock the men of his regiment received in the Great War when they first found themselves opposed to British troops. They had been told by their superiors that the British were effete and cowardly, and being simple souls they believed it. It was, therefore, with no little dismay and chagrin that they came to realize at the very first encounter the enormity of the deception that had been practised upon them.

When troops are assured that the facts are so and so, and they are suddenly confronted with a situation that is exactly the opposite to what was represented, the element of surprise is often great enough to contain all the ingredients that go to the making of a first-class panic. It cannot be too strongly emphasized that if troops are to fight with confidence they must be told the worst as well as the best.

Another powerful antidote to the instinct of fear is the craving to be important. Lord Wavell points out that "Napoleon did not gain the position he did so much by a study of rules and strategy as by a profound knowledge of human nature in war. A story of him in his early days shows his knowledge of psychology. When an artillery officer at the siege of Toulon he built a battery in such an exposed position that he was told he would never find men to hold it. He put up a placard, *The battery of men without fear*, and it was always manned."

Every man wants to be considered a hero. Weapons may change from generation to generation but human nature remains unaltered. Each battalion—and equivalent formation—should have a motto on similar lines, devised by the men themselves. No matter how extravagant it may be the troops will make every effort to live up to it if it is their own. Both in the field and in training it should constantly be impressed upon them that as a group their reputation is high and unsullied.

Needless to say, officers and non-commissioned officers must set an example in their own conduct. Hall points out that during the Great War shell-shock was from three to four times as common among officers as it was among other ranks, and he explains this disproportion by stating that "officers must not only be brave but set examples to their men."

The whole group leans upon the officer, but there is no one upon whom *he* can lean. He stands on his own feet, and if he tries to stand on the feet of someone else his prestige is immediately destroyed. Under the stress of danger his men will instinctively look in his direction, and if he shows the slightest sign of breaking their fighting power will at once diminish even if it does not collapse. But if he appears cool and collected they will fight on in the satisfaction that he has the situation well in hand.

It is when troops realize their inferiority that they can no longer be depended upon. So long as he feels that his equipment is as good as that of his opponent, the British soldier does not show much concern in regard to numerical odds. Starting with the frank conviction that he is as good as any three foreigners he continues in some astonishing fashion to justify it. At heart he is an optimist, and optimism leads to power, whilst pessimism leads to weakness.

The whole art of handling men may be summed up in the formula: Make them think optimistically. When men find their comforts neglected and feel conscious that they are badly-led they think pessimistically—and their efficiency evaporates. And when they are well-cared for, and perceive that their leaders are men who will never let them down they think optimistically—and their efficiency is increased. For optimistic thinking has a regenerative influence, whilst fear has a destructive influence. To paraphrase Napoleon's maxim: One contented man is worth three discontented men.

A soldier's greatest moral need is conviction, and never was this more true than it is today when men's minds are heavy with the uncertainty of what lies ahead. After the war will there still be jobs to go round? Will homes still be left standing? Will wives and children still be alive and unharmed in body and mind? What is the world of the future going to be like? These are questions which are occupying the minds of all thoughtful men in the services, and everything must be done that can be done to bring assurance and encouragement.

Religion can do a great deal, and if the opportunity were properly grasped it could do all. But the subject is a national and interdenominational one, and as such is almost insuperable. Meanwhile service chaplains, and the lay workers of those religious organizations which are privileged to minister to the forces, must seize hold of every opportunity to give men confidence in themselves and in their cause. Church parades can—and must—be an inspiration that will sustain men through their working days: hymns, lessons and sermons must be of a rousing and confident character.

"Thou art the Lord our God, and we are thy people." This gospel must be constantly preached. The British Empire will triumph with the help of God. This is a gospel which cannot fail to restore certainty and respect. And, moreover, it is true.

CHAPTER THIRTEEN

THE PSYCHOLOGY OF DISCIPLINE

The newly-appointed leader is likely to regard discipline as keeping a group of people in order. "Is he a good disciplinarian?" is a question that is often asked about officers and non-commissioned officers. What is discipline? How is it applied? What kind of person is the ideal disciplinarian?

Reference to a good dictionary will show that *discipline* is made up of *disciple* and *ine*. A disciple is a learner. Discipline is: (*a*) Systematic training, exercise, development and control of the mental, moral and physical faculties; and (*b*) System of instruction and control, inculcating submission to established authority; self-control, orderly behaviour.

When we say, then, that a disciplinarian is one who can keep a group of people in order we speak the truth. But that truth is after all only half the truth. A good disciplinarian is one who can influence a group of people to keep themselves in order.

Discipline is generally confused with compulsion, for compulsion is an instrument which established authority naturally turns to: the parent, the teacher, the State, the Church—each of these finds it easy and convenient to say in effect, "Do *so-and-so*, or else—!" Established authority is able to wield a club—sometimes physical and sometimes moral—that lends support to its commands. But the most elementary experience of life proves that the effects of compulsion last exactly as long as the physical or moral club can be applied.

A good leader should aim at nothing less than the highest; and the highest type of discipline is the capacity for self-control. It is not sufficient to receive a man into the army and convert him into a good fighting machine. There are other and higher objects than that. The good leader will naturally regard the army as a noble profession, and make it his consistent aim to raise the whole tone of the men who form it, to draw out their best qualities, and to give them every opportunity of earning for themselves that self-respect out of which spring all other qualities worth possessing. Discipline is more necessary to a soldier than to anyone else in the world; but there is a vast difference between the discipline which restricts and irritates, and the discipline which exists as a useful incentive.

When Lord Roberts was appointed Commander-in-Chief in India nearly sixty years ago there was one pressing matter to which he turned his immediate attention. As a newly-joined subaltern he had watched with horror the public flogging of some men belonging to his battery, and it had not taken long for his sharp wits to realize that constant punishment hardened a soldier and made him indifferent to the character he bore in the regiment. Immediately he found himself in the position of a supreme commander he issued stern orders to all concerned on the whole subject of discipline and punishment, and insisted that leniency should take the place of cut-and-dried sentences.

"I urged," he says, "that in the first two or three years of a soldier's service every allowance should be made for youth and inexperience." More than that, he gave his troops an incentive to good behaviour: he insisted on many inducements being held out to those men who kept their names clear of the defaulters' roll, and granted them privileges such as passes and more freedom generally. These wise concessions led to such revolutionary results that the list was extended. What thousands of "stern disciplinarians" had been unable to do with all their shootings, floggings and imprisonments over a period of centuries Roberts accomplished in four years by the exercise of common sense.

History seems not to have appreciated that in addition to being an outstanding soldier Roberts was a pioneer in social reform. Half a century ago drunkenness was still the worst of all social evils, and all that legislators and magistrates could do was without any lasting effect. Ninety per cent of all crime in the army was due directly or indirectly to drink. Roberts was no crank: he was fully alive to the fact that a man is none the worse because he likes a glass of beer; but he set himself to break his troops of the habit of hard drinking, and his plan was the wise one of checking an evil by putting something good in its place. It was he who started in every regiment a Soldiers' Institute where the men could read their newspapers, play their games, eat their suppers, and buy all the little extras which the soldier now takes for granted. Beer was there, too, for those who wanted it; but as the Commander-in-Chief had anticipated the men began to spend a large proportion of their pay on other things when these were placed within their reach. It is no exaggeration to say that Roberts must have saved the national exchequer some millions of pounds by his social reforms in the army, for these have done more than anything else to abolish crime, and have had a no less salutary effect in regard to disease.

Nor have such methods succeeded only in the army. Half a century ago the birch, or cane, was a prominent feature in every school in England. In those days a boy was likely to receive at the hands of his schoolmaster a far greater flogging for inattention during a lesson period than he receives nowadays from his father for shop-breaking. Every male teacher spent a considerable part of his working hours in belabouring the rising generation, not from any ill-feeling, but because it was commonly and seriously believed that flogging drove out the devil, and permitted virtue—in the form of knowledge—to enter in. Needless to say, truancy was taken for granted.

Today the cane has all but vanished and truancy is no more. The die-hards will go on maintaining that because floggings are not of such frequent performance as in their young days modern youth is going to the dogs. But juvenile crime today is only a fraction of what it was a generation ago. And never was the standard of education so high as now. Those octogenarian magistrates and other smart-alicks who profess to bewail the educational degeneracy of the times have only to compare the examination papers of their own youth with those of today in order to realize the sweeping progress that has been made.

Why has the cane disappeared from so many schools? In *Modern Education*, Dr. Raymont supplies the answer. It is because "slavery has been replaced by discipleship: plays, concerts, games, camps, and all that makes school a great piece of team work."

That statement is so very important that it must be repeated. Truancy has been abolished, juvenile crime has decreased out of all recognition, child life is a thousand times happier than it was because "*slavery has been replaced by discipleship*: plays, concerts, games, camps, and all that makes school a *great piece of team work.*"

Teachers and pupils are now brought into contact in places other than the class-room. They have a joint interest in games, concerts and other social activities. They know each other as human beings and not only as teachers and pupils. And because they know each other, and are members of the same team, they trust each other and have an affection for each other, so that the old system of discipline by compulsion is resorted to only by those who lack the initiative to study and exploit new methods.

When the members of a group are inspired by the team spirit, and feel they are at one with each other, they have a personal reason for not offending against the rules, for no man wishes to offend against himself. Nor will any man willingly offend against a leader whom he knows and respects, and whose good opinion he values. More than that, it is not easy for the most churlish of leaders to be harsh and unreasonable with a man whom he knows, and for whose welfare he is genuinely concerned.

It ought now to be obvious that the best type of discipline will evolve from the following conditions:

(1) When the leader *knows* the individuals who make up his group.
(2) When the individuals who make up the group *know* the leader.
(3) When the leader identifies himself with the group in every possible way.
(4) When the whole group is a team inspired by the enthusiasm of the leader.
(5) When the team has a high standard of *esprit de corps*.
(6) When the team is well-instructed, keen and efficient.

If these conditions can be fulfilled, and they are by no means impossible of fulfilment, crime will disappear, training will progress by leaps and bounds, men will be fighting keen, and detention barracks will be forced out of business. Proof? The best type of educationist under infinitely worse conditions—he has his team only six hours a day for five days a week, and loses it completely for long periods at a stretch—has performed far greater miracles in the slums of our great cities.

A generation ago it was common for boys to slink around the nearest corner when they saw their teachers coming along the street. Today it is a common thing for boys to lie in wait for their teachers and escort them to school. Which is the healthier attitude?

Which is the more efficient method: Slavery or discipleship?

*   *   *

Discipline is best developed by methods that are expressive rather than repressive. When discipline is merely repressive men become lazy and shifty immediately they find themselves beyond the reach of detection or punishment. They lose all power of personal initiative and honesty. They require constant supervision, and have to be driven instead of being led. Such a system is uneconomical, for it has to be supported by a vast and expensive organization that contributes nothing to an army's fighting strength and efficiency: military prisons, detention barracks, prison staff, military police, extra medical staff, extra regimental guards, extra equipment, etc.

To be efficient and powerful an army must be well-disciplined, and discipline in the group had far better evolve from discipline in the individual. Discipline is not really gained by punishing something wrong, but by influencing individuals to do what is right.

A man who is forced to disobey a command to do something impossible will soon fall into the way of disobeying a command that is within his powers. The soldier must be taught thoroughly how to do a thing before he is ordered to do it. And it must be recognized that some men are slower than others in grasping what is required of them. A drill movement must be shown repeatedly step by step. All the details which go to the making up of a tidy kit must be gone through again and again. If a machine gun has to be assembled by a recruit under instruction an instructor has no right to put some unfortunate individual in the wrong, and give him a false sense of inferiority, because he is not as mechanically-minded as others. Every instructor must keep the word *patience* constantly in mind. Human beings make the most rapid progress when they are not flustered.

It is true that ignorance of orders is no excuse for their not being obeyed: but at the same time it is absolutely unreasonable to expect a newly-joined soldier, for instance, to discover things for himself, and when he fails to discover them to punish him so that he will be more zealous in the future. The better and more efficient way is to give him habits of finding out what he is supposed to know. So long as a soldier has a clean conduct sheet he will move heaven and earth to keep it clean; but once it records a crime—no matter how trivial—his incentive to keep himself out of trouble has been destroyed. Therefore no officer ought to assume to himself the grave responsibility of destroying that incentive without a cast-iron reason.

In his useful and delightful book, *Running a Big Ship on Ten Commandments*, the late Captain Rory O'Conor, R.N., wrote: "The dignity of a great service like ours requires that every officer and man shall be given credit in the first place for doing his best, and when he sins, of sinning in ignorance or forgetfulness. Then, if he still fails, those in authority can afford to act calmly, seeing they are backed by the authority of the whole Service and the Naval Discipline Act, with the Lords Spiritual and Temporal and all the Commons in support."

Those noble words ought to be copied out and taken to heart by every officer who is called upon to administer military law.

It is not being suggested that discipline must never be repressive. Indeed, if a leader finds himself appointed to a group which he has reason to suspect is somewhat out of hand, he would be well advised to put on a bold front and take the offensive at once. No great harm will be done if for a time he is thought to be severe. Once he has been sized up as a man who knows his business it is simple enough to let out the reins. If need be they can be pulled in again later, but this necessity is not likely to arise.

The important thing to be remembered is that it is impossible to pull in reins that have been handed over to the horse. For that reason not one single mistake must ever be allowed to pass unchecked. Not one solitary misdemeanour must be passed over in silence. Not one single liberty must be taken without its being instantly rebuked. If these things are permitted or winked at the group will be completely out of hand within a few days. Small signs must be watched for and rigorously dealt with, and the large ones will never occur.

This, indeed, is the most important lesson a disciplinarian has to learn. The general temptation is to overlook the small things in the fond belief that the group will acknowledge the friendly gesture and avoid giving offence in more serious matters. But this is a disastrous fallacy. If a unit has an outbreak of serious crime then it is fairly safe to assume that one of the reasons is that small offences are not being checked: slovenliness in turn-out, unpunctuality, etc.

Here is the disciplinarian's golden rule:

Take care of the small things and the big things will take care of themselves.

In regard to the subject of punishment it must be remembered that the individuals who are being dealt with are grown men, and not undeveloped children. To punish is the most serious act one man can commit against another, and the subject deserves to be approached in a serious manner.

Beccaria, the great eighteenth-century reformer who laid the foundation of all modern criminal codes, has these precepts on crime and punishment which are as true now as when they were written.

1. Crimes are more surely prevented by the certainty than by the severity of punishments.

2. The countries most noted for the severity of punishments are always those in which the most bloody and inhuman actions are committed, for the hand of the assassin and of the legislator are directed by the same spirit of ferocity.

3. An immediate punishment is always the more useful.
4. Crime is often caused by the laws themselves.
5. One method of preventing crime is to reward virtue.

It must be emphasized that punishment ought never to be cut and dried lest it become a soulless formality. Each case must be adjudicated both on its own merits and in the light of what is good for the whole group. One question must be kept constantly in mind: How can the morale of the unit be best served? Sometimes indeed it can be best served by the infliction of exemplary punishment; and more often by the exercise of exceptional clemency.

There is the well-known story of Napoleon visiting his outposts alone, and finding one of his sentries asleep in the snow at his post on the edge of a wood. A study of the appropriate text books and manuals will prove conclusively that he ought to have called the non-commissioned officer in command of the guard, had the offender placed in close arrest, court-martialled and publicly shot. At home or abroad the one crime that admits of no excuse and which is visited with the severest retribution is this one. There can be no mercy for the soldier who shamefully imperils the lives of his comrades by sleeping at the post of duty. The most recently-appointed lance-corporal knows very well what Napoleon *ought* to have done.

But Napoleon was a man of genius, and geniuses are often inspired to do things that do not occur to ordinary men. He picked up the sleeping sentry's musket, placed it upon his own shoulder, and paced up and down the beat. And thus the two were found when the non-commissioned officer arrived with the relief: the sentry who had been posted still sleeping in the snow, and the Emperor guarding the post.

Who would be presumptuous enough to suggest that Napoleon's conduct was wrong—that he connived at the sentry's grave dereliction of duty? Shrewd psychologist that he was, it was marvellously right. General Sir George McMunn remarks of this incident: "None knew better than he the weariness that can overcome the soldier who has marched all day. Yet also none knew better how the story of the *Little Corporal* taking the musket rather than calling for the firing party must have flashed round the bivouacs and the marching columns next day. To genuine sympathy the Emperor must have added the flair of propaganda'."

And why not? It was his primary concern, as it is the primary concern of every commander, to get from his troops the greatest possible fighting-power and efficiency. In this case he was genius enough to see that there was a better way of achieving his end than by carrying out the letter of military law and having a man shot, and that was by ignoring the letter of military law and letting a man live who deserved to be shot.

It requires no powerful imagination to picture the tremendous moral effect this incident must have had on Napoleon's troops. Had they been required to go into action forthwith, they must have fought with a reckless ardour that would have astonished even their astute Commander-in-Chief himself. For what soldier would not willingly lay down his life in fighting the battles of such a leader? . . . Childish? Whether it is childish or not, it works. That is the important thing. There are many occasions when magnamimity pays, and a wise leader will take pains to sense them out.

Needless to say, when men first join the army they should be given a friendly talk on the whole subject of discipline and punishment in the light of their rights and privileges under the King's Regulations. The purpose of punishment should be carefully explained. That purpose is deterrent and not retributive; and in administering military law an officer must ask himself: (*a*) Is it necessary to punish at all in this case?—and if it is necessary—(b) What is the *least* punishment required?

A grave warning must be given in regard to collective punishment. For instance, at weekly inspection a particular barrack-room is not up to standard, and instead of investigating the matter in a just endeavour to find out the cause and fix the blame, all the men in the barrack-room are arbitrarily punished with extra fatigues, etc.

This is a most perilous procedure. The psychology of the group is a vastly different thing from the psychology of the individuals who make up the group, and, when the whole group believes itself to be suffering under an injustice, certain dangerous psychological elements are inevitably aroused. Collective punishment is often the cause of serious crime, for it binds men together for purposes of retaliation.

First, last, and all the time, it is necessary to think of morale. It will flourish best in an atmosphere of fairness, confidence and respect.

CHAPTER FOURTEEN

IDEALS

Under good leadership a group is greater than the sum total of its members; and under bad leadership it is less.

In *The Group Mind*, McDougall says: "It is a notorious fact that, when a number of men think and feel and act together, the mental operations and the actions of each member of the group are apt to be very different from those he would achieve if he faced the situation as an isolated individual. Hence, though we may know each member of a group so intimately that we can, with some confidence, foretell his actions under given circumstances, we cannot foretell the behaviour of the group from our knowledge of the individuals alone."

Every group begins with certain pronounced advantages and disadvantages which are inseparable from its psychology. To take the disadvantages first, one of the most serious of these is the low degree of intelligence which a group commonly exhibits. Groups of sane people forming a committee or council often come to decisions so absurdly impracticable or monstrously unjust that a disinterested observer, knowing nothing of group psychology, might be pardoned for believing that all the individuals concerned were mentally deficient. The reason for these extraordinary decisions is that in a group the least intelligent minds bring down the intelligence of the whole to their own level; and the subtle power of suggestibility does the rest.

Again, a man joining the army often brings with him certain high ideals in regard to sexual morality, religious observance, temperance, truth, honesty, etc. Within a short time—in some cases—these ideals have gone by the board: he will make no effort to fulfil what previously he regarded as his religious obligations; his language will be as foul as the language of the most depraved member of the group; he will see no harm in sexual immorality and intemperance; he will tell a lie readily to save himself from extra duty or punishment; and if he finds himself alone in the quartermaster's stores he will act like a common thief. And what is more, in each instance he will defend his conduct with a fervour that would shock his civilian friends.

Nor is it by any means uncommon for the army to be blamed for this metamorphosis. Actually, of course, it is no more to blame than when the same individual contracts influenza during an epidemic. He is the victim of group influences which are by no means peculiar to the army. It is notorious in times of peace that moral tone varies from station to station. And it is equally notorious, too, that in what the soldier calls civil life moral tone varies from factory to factory. It is not considered wrong to pilfer tools, or to lie about one's output of work. And in certain factories, where the sexes work side by side, the level of conversation is often such as would embarrass and horrify a regular soldier who had spent his life in the comparatively secluded atmosphere of the service. In any group the most depraved minds tend to reduce the general standard of morality to their own level; and, again, the subtle power of suggestibility does the rest.

A third disadvantage is that of panic. Every army punishes with death desertion in the face of the enemy, for it is universally recognized that one man possesses the terrible power to stampede an army of his comrades. There are conditions in which the bravery of the group can be contemptibly inferior to the bravery of the least inspiring member of the group.

In regard to the advantages of organized group life these are no less striking. There are conditions in which a group, actuated with a common purpose, will carry out a task with an inflexible determination and an incredible bravery of which no one of its members would be individually capable. And what might be called the impact of a well-disciplined group is infinitely greater than the impact of its members.

These advantages and disadvantages of group life call attention to the need of good leadership within the group. It is true that the intelligence of the group is inferior to the intelligence of its members. But the leader does not consult the intelligence of the group as a group, though sometimes he will find it necessary to consult the intelligence of one or two individuals. All decisions are his own, and it is reasonable to suppose that they are inspired by the highest individual intelligence which the group contains.

One important purpose of leadership is to develop and

harness the collective mind of the group so that it can work with the maximum of power and effect. In an army the collective mind is more commonly developed by rivalry—in games, training, etc.—with similar groups. The importance of this rivalry is that it binds the members of a group together, and gives them a sense of common purpose. A group which has that sense highly developed will always be more effective than one which has not.

The value and effect of this rivalry can be illustrated by an incident taken at random from British military history. During the Indian Mutiny, Sir Colin Campbell was faced with the necessity of retaking a village situated half-way between Delhi and Allahabad, as here a force of more than five thousand rebels had concentrated. Between the Highland and Irish regiments a certain amount of jealousy existed, as Sir Colin was understood to have a special affection and preference for the former, and to give them therefore the posts of danger and honour. So while the troops were waiting in readiness to attack the village, whence the enemy was pouring out a wicked fire, the Irishmen, determined to be well to the front, took the law into their own hands, and without waiting for orders dashed forward and completely cleared out the enemy. Sir Colin was furious, galloped up to the regiment and reprimanded them sharply, but all in vain, for each remark he made they drowned with a cry of "Three cheers for the Commander-in-Chief, boys!" till his anger melted away and he left them laughing.

The discipline may have been lamentable, but the *esprit de corps*—engendered by rivalry—was magnificent. When a group has both the effect is irresistible, and it is that effect which a leader must endeavour to obtain.

The moral standard of a group can be raised to a high level only when the group if actuated by high and unselfish ideals. If it is not so actuated then the moral level will certainly be lower than that of its best individuals, and the group will suffer in consequence.

Oliver Cromwell realized more than most leaders that men who are inspired by unselfish ideals will fight better than men who are not so inspired. At the battle of Edgehill he learnt that victories were won by swift and resolute attack and that assault was the only defence. His mind was full of that magic quality called fighting spirit. How could it be acquired?

To quote John Buchan: "Piety was not enough, unless it was of the militant brand, a spirit as tough and as daring as that of the King's gallant, adventurous and long-descended youth. A moral fervour must be matched against the chivalry of England."

As Cromwell had once said to Hampden: "Your troopers are most of them old decayed serving men and tapsters and such kind of fellows; and their troopers are gentlemen's sons, younger sons and persons of quality. Do you think that the spirit of such mean and base fellows will be ever able to encounter gentlemen who have honour and courage and resolution in them? You must get men of a spirit that is likely to go on as far as gentlemen will go, or else I am certain you will be beaten still."

And Edgehill convinced Cromwell that his immediate duty was a new kind of recruiting drive, to raise "Such men as had the fear of God before them and made some conscience of what they did."

In these days of vast citizen armies it is hardly possible that the land forces could be possessed with a burning moral fervour unless it were infused by, or shared with, the nation at large. The days have gone by when it was possible to separate the morale of an army from the morale of the nation. If the morale of the nation breaks, the morale of the army must also break. On the other hand, even in the twentieth century, with its long-range weapons of mass destruction, it is still possible for an army to fight with a moral fervour that cannot be resisted. An army's most powerful weapons are its ideals. But these weapons, like all the others, must be forged by the nation.

What is the common purpose which binds together the people of the British Empire during the present conflict with the Axis powers? The answer is simple: The defeat of those powers. But every thoughtful person must know that such a purpose in itself is far too commonplace. Every German believes passionately that he is fighting for his very existence, and for the existence of his nearest and dearest. For years he has been told that his enemies were encircling him with the object of choking the life out of him and finishing him off once and for all. And in the result the German is naturally fighting with the frenzy and ferocity of a drowning man.

The supreme fighting qualities of the Imperial forces must be reinforced by a powerful common purpose. Faced with the problem of finding for his army a common purpose that would make his men fight to the death, Oliver Cromwell was inspired to believe, or was psychologist enough to realize, that the most powerful common purpose an army could have was to regard itself as a divine instrument specially appointed and called forth to execute divine judgment. For what human power could withstand a divine power? Any army inspired by such a purpose must inevitably conquer.

He had forestalled Napoleon who was cautiously to declare that "Moral force to the physical is as three to one." Even if he never announced it in so many words, Cromwell had hit on the magic formula: *Divine force to the physical is as infinity to one.*

And so it proved.

In *The Souldiers Catechisme*, published in 1644, the Parliament's troops were instructed from the Word of God that: (1) Their profession was a noble one; (2) Their cause was just; (3) The war was a religious war; (4) Their enemies had persecuted religion, subverted justice, and dethroned liberty; (5) They owed it to posterity, no less than to themselves, to make a stand for things that were honest and right; (6) Those who did not share their enthusiasm and ideals were faint-hearted cowards and the secret enemies of God; (7) God himself would deal with such; (8) Their own cause must prevail because (a) it was just and good, and (b) the enemy's cause was thoroughly bad; (9) God could not support a wicked enemy; (10) A good cause had God on its side; (11) A good soldier must be religious and godly; (12) Such a soldier would be blessed by God.

When they were not fighting or training the Parliament's soldiers were engaged in searching the Scriptures and in prayer. Swearing, intemperance, and immorality were freely given up in order that the army might become a fitting instrument for the execution of the divine will. Men found themselves inspired by new ideals. And they began to win engagements instead of losing them: Gloucester, Newbury, Hull, Lincoln, Gainsborough, Nantwich and Alsford—victories such as these, they felt, were indeed evidence that God was with them. And if God was with them, who *could* stand against them?

The war was won.

It would be enough today if even a small, but organized, group of men felt themselves inspired by a common purpose no less selfless and confident. For when such a purpose is tenaciously held and passionately believed in it must inevitably flare up till it burns and spreads with the irresistible power and intensity of a forest fire.

When man is without ideals his conduct is under the control of his impulses. But when a set of ideals is firmly implanted in his soul, and his reason is satisfied that they are worth pursuing, then indeed his will is aroused and assumes the control of his conduct. Paltry ideals can inspire no enthusiasm. The greater they are and the more difficult of attainment, so much the more eagerly will men strive to attain them. The British soldier must be encouraged to be satisfied with nothing less than the highest.

This war will have been won when the Allied forces have been inspired to believe that the overthrow of the Nazi regime is a task which has been imposed upon them by the divine will.

Divine force to the physical is as infinity to one.

THE END.

For Product Safety Concerns and Information please contact our EU
representative GPSR@taylorandfrancis.com
Taylor & Francis Verlag GmbH, Kaufingerstraße 24, 80331 München, Germany

www.ingramcontent.com/pod-product-compliance
Lightning Source LLC
Chambersburg PA
CBHW070545300426
44113CB00011B/1800